Colour
Forecasting

Colour
Forecasting

Tracy Diane BSc, MA, PhD
Lecturer
Manchester Metropolitan University

&

Tom Cassidy MSc, MBA, PhD, ATI
Professor of Design
and Head of School of Design
University of Leeds

Blackwell
Publishing

Editorial Offices:
Blackwell Publishing Ltd, 9600 Garsington Road, Oxford OX4 2DQ, UK
   Tel: +44 (0)1865 776868
Blackwell Publishing Professional, 2121 State Avenue, Ames, Iowa 50014-8300, USA
   Tel: +1 515 292 0140
Blackwell Publishing Asia, 550 Swanston Street, Carlton, Victoria 3053, Australia
   Tel: +61 (0)3 8359 1011

First published 2005 by Blackwell Publishing Ltd

Library of Congress Cataloging-in-Publication Data
Diane, Tracy.
   Colour forecasting / Tracy Diane, Tom Cassidy.
        p. cm.
   Includes bibliographical references and index.
   ISBN-13: 978-1-4051-2120-0 (pbk. : alk. paper)
   ISBN-10: 1-4051-2120-3 (pbk. : alk. paper)
   1. Color in clothing.   2. Fashion—Forecasting.   I. Cassidy, Tom, Ph.D.   II. Title.

   TT507.D528 2005
   746.9′2—dc22   2004024403

ISBN-13: 978-1-4051-2120-0
ISBN-10: 1-4051-2120-3

A catalogue record for this title is available from the British Library

Set in 10/13pt Stone Sans
by Graphicraft Limited, Hong Kong
Printed and bound in India
by Replika Press Pvt Ltd, Kundli

The publisher's policy is to use permanent paper from mills that operate a sustainable forestry policy, and which has been manufactured from pulp processed using acid-free and elementary chlorine-free practices. Furthermore, the publisher ensures that the text paper and cover board used have met acceptable environmental accreditation standards.

For further information on Blackwell Publishing, visit our website:
www.blackwellpublishing.com

Contents

The authors

Dr Tracy Diane is a lecturer of Fashion Marketing at the Hollings Campus of Manchester Metropolitan University. She has held colour and forecasting as a central theme throughout her undergraduate and postgraduate education. She also teaches, holds colour workshops for industry and continues her design research activities.

Professor Tom Cassidy has 34 years experience in the textile and fashion industry and education. He is now Professor of Design and Head of the School of Design at the University of Leeds. He continues his research into the process, technology and management of design.

Foreword

Colour is one of the great joys of life, its exploration and uses never ending. Colour is involved in life, art, design, lifestyle and fashion. Fashion is colour, colour is fashion, giving feeling and emotion to ever changing trends and is an essential part of our everyday life. Colour has been an important part of our lifestyle, expression, decoration and design since the dawn of civilisation.

In today's fast moving world the scope, range and use of colour is daunting for both the consumer and the professional. Colour, design and fashion pass freely around the world, without passport or hindrance, facilitated by ever faster communication technology. The need to understand colour in all its facets has never been more important and, therefore, colour forecasting is an essential requirement to facilitate the needs and demands of this ever changing world of fashion.

Colour has very personal and emotional qualities, making forecasting new colour trends a complex process involving a combination of intuition, directional awareness and market research. Little information exists about fashion forecasting, especially compared with the literature published on colour theory and the production and application of colour. This book fills the gap in information on this subject by covering the historical aspects of colour and the theoretical areas of cutting edge colour trends and predictions. It stems from an in-depth research project on colour forecasting by the authors, Tracy Diane and Tom Cassidy. They have defined and explained colour forecasting and have presented their findings in a logical, understandable format, while explaining the myths and legends of colour forecasting by fully exploring the magic, excitement and joy of colour.

The process of colour forecasting defines the needs and demands of the consumer and the requirements of the fashion business. Therefore, this book is indispensable for fashion students and professionals, fashion and textile designers,

designers involved in lifestyle products and all who have an involvement in the world of colour.

Professor Edward Newton
Chair, Professor of Fashion Design
Institute of Textiles and Clothing
Hong Kong Polytechnic University

Acknowledgements

The authors would like to thank the many design and forecasting personnel who took part in our survey to provide validation of the process models. Also all the students and consumers who took part in the education and consumer preference investigations. Obviously there were too many people involved to name, however, we feel that the following should be thanked individually: design consultant Zina Roweth, who provided invaluable insight at the early stages of our work; Mrs Helen Dunn, of De Montfort University's Fashion Department, who offered continuous support; Professor Edward Newton of Hong Kong Polytechnic University for his encouragement; also Professor Michael Hann of the School of Design, University of Leeds; finally, Dr Gerard Moran, Dean of the Faculty of Art and Design at De Montfort University, for being there.

Introduction: what is colour forecasting?

The colour forecasting process is one of great complexity and very much an intuitive one. As yet, little information exists about its methodology, even though the process is considered to be a major driving force of the fashion and textile industry.

Colour forecasting is a fundamental part of a collective process known as fashion forecasting or trend prediction, where individuals or teams attempt to accurately forecast the colours, fabrics and styles of fashionable garments and accessories that consumers will purchase in the near future, approximately two years ahead.

The process of colour forecasting is basically one of collecting, evaluating, analysing and interpreting data to anticipate a range of colours desirable by the consumer, using a strong element of intuition, inspiration and creativity.

A dichotomy exists around opinions as to whether or not the forecaster predicts trends or merely creates them. Either way, a process has evolved over a period of time which has, in more recent decades, become increasingly complex. So much so that the secondary resource material readily available to the fashion student rarely offers more than a brief outline of the concept, the tools and the basic methodology involved in the colour and fashion forecasting process.

The process of colour and fashion forecasting has become a more integral part of the roles of many within the industry. Designers, range developers, sourcing personnel, buyers and merchandisers – and especially those who specialise in trend prediction for the purpose of selling their prediction packages to the industry – all use the current forecasting system. It is becoming increasingly important to clarify this process, both for those currently using the system and for the newcomer to forecasting, in order to improve forecasting.

While fashion forecasting incorporates all aspects of the design of garments and accessories, colour is a significant factor for the consumer when making a purchasing decision.

It is therefore considered that the colour forecasting process is a worthwhile subject to be investigated and further understood in its own right.

Colour forecasting is a specialist sector activity. This specialist sector is a service that makes use of the colour forecasting process. The information is compiled into trend prediction packages and sold to the fashion and textile industry. Personnel within the industry use this information for direction, suggestion and as a source of inspiration. They then use the same process – or a very similar one – to develop their own company's colour range. This book concentrates on the process applied to the development of colour stories or ranges from the specialist sector throughout the various sectors of the fashion and textile industry. However, discussions with our friends and colleagues in the product design, interior design and paint industries suggest that the information provided would be more widely welcomed.

Manufacturers use the prediction packages as one source of data together with other data collected. They then apply the colour forecasting process, or a version of it, to formulate their own seasonal colour ranges for their products to sell to the retail sector. The retailers may also subscribe to the colour forecasting services, purchasing the prediction packages to use as a source of inspiration to assist them to formulate their colour ranges.

Consumers use a process of decision making when selecting a garment to purchase. Colour preferences are an extremely influential aspect taken into consideration. Successful sales reflect the effectiveness of the colour decisions that were made throughout the industry.

The concept of forecasting came about through the development and growth of the fashion and textile industry to enable manufacturers to produce end products that would create sales on the high street. By the latter half of the twentieth century, a greater need had developed for more accurate information to be readily available to all sectors of the industry, from fibre, yarn and fabric manufacturers, through to the garment manufacturers and retailers – collectively known as the fashion and textile industry. As the industry developed globally and consumer lifestyles became more varied, so the process of collecting the necessary data for forecasting became increasingly diverse and complex.

Seasonal colours have become a powerful driving force of fashion today. The colour forecasting service was developed to fill a communication gap between the primary market manufacturers and the consumer, recognising the increasing complexities of forecasting with advances in marketing strategies.

The service was established to deal with the problem of anticipating the colour demand/preferences of the consumer prior to the industry's production time plan (lead time), thereby unburdening manufacturers of this process. While the concept of forecasting was originally for the primary market sector, selling information to the secondary and tertiary market sectors increased the revenue for the service sector and influenced a stronger consensus for the conviction of the colour stories. Whatever colours are finally predicted for a season and however these colours are promoted throughout the industry to the consumer, it is the decision to purchase made by the consumer that determines whether or not the predictions were accurate or valid. Marketing may influence the consumer's decision to buy; however, the colour choice is still the decision of the consumer, based upon their personal preferences.

As the fashion and textile industry is currently changing, retailers are showing evidence of relaying their observations and evaluation of the needs of the consumer back to the manufacturers, shifting the influence on colour direction from the manufacturer to the retailers. Developments in mass customisation suggest that the current forecasting process is not as effective or successful as the industry would like. As the customer now is to some extent – and possibly always will be – a major driving force of fashion, their preferences are a key aspect for consideration.

Aims and objectives

The aim of this book is to demystify the colour forecasting process, and to provide a better understanding of its methodology. Through the development of process models we attempt to develop a potential improvement to forecasting, though there is no intention whatsoever on our part to dismiss the importance and relevance of intuition and inspiration as an integral part of the process.

The main objectives of the book are:

- to improve understanding of the current colour forecasting process
- to develop an appreciation of how, when and why the need for colour and fashion forecasting came about, and how the current colour forecasting process evolved
- to establish who the forecasters are, how they develop colour stories, and how this information is used by the industry
- to examine the methodologies hidden behind the mystique of the colour forecasting profession
- to investigate other methodologies that could be applied to the current process of colour forecasting
- to devise models of the current system and of a proposed improved system
- to test developed models to assess their validity
- to develop an understanding of consumer preference data and its potential benefit to the current system.

In this book

We shall develop our understanding of the colour forecasting process, its importance in the industry and the potential to improve the current system, employing the concept of consumer colour preference data or consumer colour acceptability.

Chapter summaries

Chapter 1: Fashion forecasting and the driving forces of fashion: 1700–2000

In this chapter you will explore the development of the fashion and textile industry from the onset of the industrial revolution until the present day. The main aim here is to identify the driving forces of fashion throughout history, as these influences are key aspects that have directed the development of the forecasting sector that exists in today's industry.

Chapter 2: The views of forecasters and trend information users

In this chapter you will be introduced to the language of forecasters and to the fundamental process of forecasting. You will be made aware of varying attitudes towards the process and the importance of forecasting within the industry – from those actually involved in it. You will learn the importance of colour forecasting to the industry and the methods that forecasters use. The skills of forecasting will be discussed and also the important aspects of colour and colour forecasting.

Chapter 3: Colour knowledge

The workshop approach to this chapter will enable you to experiment with colour mixing and colour schemes in order to understand colour and its application in the forecasting process. There will be discussions of the historical background of colour learning, including colour light, vision and additive colour mixing. The colour wheel will be introduced and discussed to develop an understanding of subjective colour mixing. Colour terminology used by forecasters and its mean-ing will be explained, and colour schemes will be worked through. This chapter is supported by a colour workshop that will be instrumental for you in developing and experimenting with colour mixing and colour combinations.

Chapter 4: The colour forecasting process

Through this chapter you will increase your knowledge of the colour forecasting process currently used in the fashion and textile industry. We will discuss strengths and weaknesses of the process with a view to improvement, and introduce you to a deeper understanding of the process through a conceptual model that has been tested and refined through an extensive survey of the industry. The role of colour throughout the supply chain is highlighted. The effectiveness of this model is evaluated and compared to the expectations of the forecasters and a revised second conceptual model is also included with re-searched assessments of how this model could be an im-provement to the current system. The role of the consumer and the possible benefits to the consumer will also be discussed.

Chapter 5: The colour forecaster's tool kit

Discussions in this chapter will assist you in achieving a highly developed understanding of the more subjective tools that are of such importance in the colour forecasting process. Information is provided about the individual components of the process, including its strengths and weaknesses. Intuition, inspiration, thought, reasoning and decision-making processes are shown to be necessary adjuncts to other forecasting tools. These aspects are discussed with reference to their application to the process and their context within the model. This chapter also provides the foundation for the discussions and experimental elements of the next chapter.

Chapter 6: Colour story development and presentation

This chapter looks deeper into the methodology and application of the current colour forecasting process. Teaching methods are discussed and we also consider how students approach the task of mood board and colour range development, looking at the thought, reasoning and decision-making procedures that forecasters apply to their working methodology. You will learn about the fundamental approaches through a structured workshop type discussion and experimentation to develop a deep understanding of how to produce and evaluate a well designed mood board and achieve a high standard of presentation.

Chapter 7: The future of colour forecasting

In this final chapter you will be introduced to aspects for consideration as additions to the present forecasting process, in order to provide greater benefit to the industry and consumer. This will encourage possible future research projects that may add to the current body of colour forecasting knowledge. This chapter concludes the book with a summary of what you have learnt and the importance of this book's contribution.

This is the first book to explain fully the process that colour forecasters use to compile trend prediction information. This complex and intuitive process is discussed objectively, establishing and assessing the process as a whole before rigorously interpreting the highly subjective individual components. The strengths and weaknesses of the current method are identified and discussed, and suggestions made with a view to improving the system through surveying the industry in order to test process models defined in Chapter 4. The refined models included and discussed are useful for all aspects of fashion trend prediction, not just for colour forecasting. An extremely valuable section (in Chapter 6) is included for you to both understand the colour forecasting process more clearly and also to develop your own creative skills for mood board development and develop presentation skills to a high standard. This is a fundamentally important aspect of fashion and textile related degree courses, as well as for the colour forecasting process. There is also a discussion on teaching approaches to colour forecasting and the need for colour knowledge amongst design students and practitioners.

Fashion forecasting and the driving forces of fashion: 1700–2000

Before trying to understand the process of colour forecasting, it is helpful to explore the historical development of the fashion and textile industry. This will demonstrate how a series of events influenced the need for forecasting trends and how this need in turn affected the evolution of the forecasting process. We will show when and why forecasting colour and fashion direction became a necessity for the industry. By identifying the driving forces of fashion past and present, it is easier to understand how and why the colour forecasting process was started and developed to its present day state.

The period from 1700 to 2000 is a useful one to study fashion directions as it includes the years just prior to the industrial revolution, as well as the revolution itself. Many existing textbooks give accounts of the technical developments in the textile and garment production and related industries since the industrial revolution. Likewise, much information is readily available on the history of fashion. If you are interested in studying these areas in more detail, the bibliography at the back of this book is a good source of further reading.

The eighteenth century

It is often assumed that the initial driving force of fashion was the development of the cotton industry during the 1730s, with the invention of Kay's flying shuttle (which made the mechanised loom and mass production of woven fabrics possible) followed by cotton-spinning machinery. Examining developments from the beginning of the century, however, reveals that the first spinning machines were actually for the

In this chapter

We shall explore the development of the fashion and textile industry, from the onset of the industrial revolution to the present day. The main aim of this chapter is to identify the driving forces of fashion as these key influences determine the development of today's forecasting sector. Significant inventions and developments in the textile and garment production industry are categorised and we:

- identify the true driving forces of fashion
- explain both the importance of forecasting fashion direction and its peculiarities.

spinning of silk. At this time silk and cotton fabrics were imported into Britain and could be afforded only by the wealthy. Silk had the aesthetic advantage of its luxurious appearance but also had other characteristics such as good handling qualities and 'drapability', as well as excellent dyeing potential, enabling brighter colours to be produced than were achievable at that time on woollen fabrics. This made silk fabrics much sought after by the wealthier classes. The mass population, on the other hand, could barely afford the cheap wool fabrics that were increasingly available as a result of the new machines.

Manufacturing

The ability to spin silk in Britain brought down the price of silk fabrics. It is likely that this inspired the development of spinning methods in Britain for cotton. Indeed, it may have been predicted that the cheap production of cotton would make the more expensive fabrics affordable, not only to the wealthier classes of society but also to the poor, thereby increasing the volume of production for the manufacturer. The spinning industry improved the speed and quality of yarn production in Britain, making higher quality yarns abundantly available. As the weaving entrepreneurs developed weaving looms that increased the rate of fabric production, the textile industry began to expand. Knitting frames were first invented during the sixteenth century but had been little refined until this time. Now, improvements to these machines boosted the hosiery trade. Cotton fabrics were easier to wash than wool, as they could be boiled and were therefore considered more hygienic. This helped to stimulate the demand for cotton fabrics while improvements in production methods and machinery increased their availability. Until this time, spinning, weaving and knitting activities had been undertaken within the home by family members in what is now known as a 'cottage industry'. The new machines were much larger than the home could accommodate and as a result, mills and factories steadily replaced the home as the workplace.

The driving forces of fashion

The opening of more and more spinning mills and fabric manufacturing factories produced an era of businessmen and increased entrepreneurship. As more wealth circulated, class division became ever more apparent. The wealthy began to set the unwritten (but much adhered to) rules of social status and acceptable behaviour. Women's dress, i.e. that of wives and daughters became a symbol of a man's wealth and social position. As fabrics became cheaper to produce and more readily available to the mass population, the upper classes saw the status gap reduce as far as appearance through fashion was concerned. Therefore style, cut and fit became more important to high fashion, which encouraged the development of skilled labour in this small manufacturing sector. Styles varied much during the eighteenth century, from the more practical styles of the early decades to wide gowns utilising hoops, then back to the slimmer styles of the latter decades. The first recognised designer of this time was Rose Bertin. She opened her salon in Paris in 1773, closing some 20 years later. She gained a reputation for having a rare talent for colour, style and fit and later became dressmaker to Queen Marie Antoinette.

By the end of the century, the garment manufacturing process within the fashion industry came into being with the development of the early sewing machines. Many inventions and patents for sewing machines were recorded from the mid-eighteenth century onwards. Most of these early machines were designed to imitate hand sewing; the first patented machine not to imitate this action was that of Thomas Saint in 1790, a replica of which was produced by Rogerson in 1873. The better-known sewing machine

manufacturer, Singer, entered the market in 1851 and produced the first domestic machine in 1856. Singer continued
to develop machines for both the industrial and domestic
sewing machine markets. As the mechanisation of fibre preparation and of yarn and fabric production accelerated, so
the garment manufacturing process followed suit. Also at
this time magazines were becoming available specifically for
women. These often included fashion notes, illustrations
known as 'colour engravings' of the day's fashion and tips for
ladies to share with their dressmakers.

The early nineteenth century

By the 1800s the garment manufacturing industry was more
concerned with improving the machinery and the production
techniques than with further new inventions. Factories were
also by now well established, taking production away from
the cottage industry.

The driving forces of fashion

By the beginning of the nineteenth century social class and
status were firmly established. The division of wealth was by
now so great between the classes that efforts had shifted from
maintaining class division away from the middle and lower
classes to within the upper class. Many fashion history books
tell of how George Byran 'Beau' Brummell relished outdoing
his good friend the Prince Regent in terms of fashion and
image, which inspired high quality standards in British tailoring. This penetrated into the upper class circles of socialites,
determined to outdo their acquaintances and business associates by displaying their wealth. The frivolity of upper class
women at this time provided fashion with its most powerful
driving force to date. The development of the textile industry
now simply served as a support to the extravagances of
fashion to come.

Social events became important to facilitate the display of
wealth. Fashion historians suggest that a new gown would have
been considered necessary for each occasion. Second-hand
clothing or hand-me-downs were passed down through

the classes, from the original wearers to their maids and eventually finding their way to the lower classes. This would further exacerbate the need to have more frequent changes in fashion to separate the highly fashionable, up-to-date wealthy man's wife from the lower classes' out-of-date styles.

Heavier plush fabrics and velvets were now available to the wealthier classes due to the growth of the textile industry but fabrics alone could no longer distinguish the classes, as a wider variety of fabrics were increasingly affordable and readily available to the masses. This allowed them to copy the fashions of high society, which were by now widely published in a large selection of women's magazines. These too, would find their way to the lower classes as old copies were handed down.

Early fashion forecasting

By 1825 lightweight wool blend fabrics were widely produced in Britain after some manufacturers had visited the USA and were inspired by these fabrics used for outerwear. This could be the earliest indication of a need for forecasting fashion direction by the manufacturers as well as evidence of taking inspiration from further afield – abroad. This method of inspiration is still part of the modern day forecasting process. As early as 1828 fashion styles were promoted in the French magazine, *La Bella Assemblée* which did not become a popular feature of fashion until a decade later. Remember that fashion changes were slow at this time, so it is difficult in this instance to differentiate between what may have been early forecasting, and a source of inspiration on the part of the designer.

The mid-nineteenth century

By the mid-nineteenth century more developments were slowly taking place in all areas of the manufacturing sector, to further improve production rate and quality. The invention of the latch needle for the knitting frame in 1849 developed by Matthew Townsend played a pivotal role in the revolution of the knitting industry. The specialist industry that had evolved supplying the wealthier classes known now as 'bespoke' due to its one-to-one design-consultancy approach was also growing rapidly as more wealth became available.

Nineteenth century fashion designers

In 1842, John Redfern opened his tailoring business in Paris, followed by Henry Creed in 1850 and Charles Worth in 1858. While today Redfern is considered to be one of the first designers to be established, we must not forget Rose Bertin as previously mentioned. Paris probably became the early fashion centre because of the excellent French silk industry established in Lyons; silk was still the most important high fashion fabric at the time. Worth is considered the first designer to have had a great influence upon the fashion world, though this is more likely to be due to his astute business strategies than to his talent as a designer.

Now that fashions were more readily available to and affordable by the masses, they were freely disseminated in magazines along with garment production notes, making fashionable dress-making at home more possible. The second-hand clothing trade recycled high fashion garments, making them easier to obtain by the lower classes. The only way to ensure distinction between the classes was through style, cut and fit. Worth exploited the capriciousness of the wealthy woman with new marketing methods. He introduced the concept of clients coming to him, instead of the designer going to the client's home. His wife became the first live model displaying his works and he commonly turned ladies away from his establishment, refusing to design for them, which served to make his designs exclusive and even more sought after.

Department stores and ready-to-wear clothing

Harrods, originally a grocery store, was established in London in 1849 as Europe's largest department store selling a wide range of products. By the mid-nineteenth century, department stores were becoming a common feature of major towns and cities, offering a one-stop-shop as the product range could be seen to provide for almost all of the consumers' needs. They played a fundamental part in the dissemination of fashion and the establishment of the ready-to-wear industry. Improvements to the sewing machine and its increased use in the industry also encouraged the ready-to-wear industry to develop quickly throughout Britain. This followed Brooks Brothers of New York, recognised as the pioneer of the ready-to-wear clothing industry in the USA, having established off-the-peg tailoring for menswear in 1818, primarily without the use of the sewing machine. Department stores in Britain displayed part-made garments that were completed bespoke for the customer, within the store's workshop.

Colour

In 1862, an international exhibition was held in London showing fabrics in the new colours now available as developments in the dyeing industry had accelerated since Perkin's discovery of synthetic dyes, in the mid-1850s. Developments in fibre preparation, and yarn and fabric production had by now slowed down, with emphasis shifting to improving existing methods.

Man-made fibre development

The two fashion fabric industries – silk and cotton – had both suffered set-backs in the mid-nineteenth century; silk by the disease of silk worms in France, and cotton by the American Civil War 1861 to 1865. These events may have accelerated the development of synthetic fibres, as the first cellulose acetate was developed as early as 1866. By 1869, cellulose acetate yarns and fabrics were being produced in Germany.

Garment production

During the latter half of the nineteenth century, the sewing machine became more commonly used in the clothing industry, and demand from the wealthy forced high fashion styles to become more intricate in order to signal their class status. This gave handmade bespoke garments the cutting edge over the fast growing ready-to-wear industry, now increasingly popular for the lower classes, even though the quality was not very high.

By the early 1870s paper patterns were also readily available through fashion magazines and mail order operations. Paper pattern companies were started up. Butterick opened its first paper pattern shop in 1873, followed in 1879 by McCall who had originally established themselves in the market through magazines in 1870. Both companies were well established in Britain as well as in the USA. Other influences came from the entertainment world with actresses such as Lillie Langtry, who promoted the designs of Redfern in the early 1870s.

The late nineteenth century

Jacques Doucet, another important nineteenth century designer, opened his couture house in 1875. Couture houses were popular establishments for actresses, royalty, the aristocracy and wealthy socialites to frequent.

By the 1880s, sports such as golf, tennis, croquet and skating were becoming increasingly popular pastimes for the wealthy, both men and women, followed by cycling in the 1890s. This sports boom created a new direction for the knitwear industry. Until then, most knitted fabrics produced by machine were for the hosiery industry. Recent advances in the automation of knitting frames and patterning devices enabled the increasing demand for knitwear, particularly sweaters, to be met.

During the remainder of the nineteenth century, many more fashion houses opened in Paris and London. Madame Paquin was another designer who, like Worth, developed and utilised early techniques for the effective marketing of fashion. She opened her Paris house in 1891 and is considered to have been the first female fashion designer of any significance. Like Worth, this is likely to have been due to her business acumen as opposed to her design talent.

Developments in the dyeing and finishing industries were stimulated and subsequently demonstrated through international exhibitions, where new colours were displayed.

By the end of the nineteenth century, fashion magazines were still a crucial vehicle for the dissemination of high fashion and also became significant in suggesting future fashion directions. The department store increased its role in making fashions more readily available to all classes and production processes continued to improve. Paris had become an important place for manufacturers to visit for the purchase of garments, or models, as they were called, to copy and sell.

The early twentieth century

By the turn of the twentieth century, the rigid class distinctions in behaviour slowly started to relax. After the death of Queen Victoria in 1901, Britain began to shed its mourning dress and the associated sombre colours that had dominated for some 40 years since the death of Prince Albert.

Technical developments

Much research was now being undertaken in the man-made fibre field. Fabrics such as Courtauld's viscose rayon, developed between 1900 and 1904, had a monopoly within the industry by 1914. A similar position was reached by British Celanese Ltd in the 1920s with their acetate. Originally these fibres were designed to imitate silk but later they became important in their own right, with their own special characteristics. Synthetic dyeing processes were well developed by now, with the inclusion of metal complex dyes (1900–1915) for silk and wool fibres; azoic dyes (1912) for synthetic fibres; and natural cellulosic fibres, i.e. cotton and disperse dyes (1920) for acetate. Overlocking machines with trim devices, first established in the knitwear industry in 1889, were now widely in use assisting the cut-and-sew process for knitwear fabrics, which further increased productivity.

Fashion dissemination

Black and white photography, first used in 1890, contributed to the dissemination of fashion in 1924–1925, as the photo-tone process enabled reproduction in magazines and other paper-based media, such as newspapers and mail order brochures. From 1932, holiday travel became an important pastime for the wealthy. Fashion dissemination was possible now through post cards, which originated in 1901–1902 and cigarette cards, which were first circulated in the 1890s. The Gibson Girl, 1890–1910, was the creation of American illustrator, Charles Dana Gibson, who captured fashion styles and the ideology of femininity. The Gibson Girl featured on many of the collectable cigarette cards and became an advertiser of fashion, and in 1904, Camille Clifford portrayed the Gibson Girl on stage. Couture houses began to sell ideas of fashion to the ready-to-wear industry, increasing their importance as a source of inspiration.

The ready-to-wear industry

Innovative manufacturers of ready-to-wear garments began to push the frontiers of fashion forward by seeking inspiration from the couture ranges in order to meet the demands of the lower to middle classes. One example of this was the addition of slits and pleats to the 'hobble skirt', so named as its slim tubular, ankle-length form made walking so difficult that the wearer hobbled. This encouraged improvements in quality as well the search for more profitable marketing avenues.

As the ready-to-wear retail sector grew and lifestyles became more diverse, it became more difficult for manufacturers to read and meet the needs and desires of the consumer. This became evident during the 1920s, when attempts to reintroduce ankle-length skirts were unsuccessful. This was because most women still preferred the less restricting length that sat just below the knee. This style enabled freedom of movement, particularly important for the popular dance craze 'ragtime' as jazz music gained popularity. Later, during the 1930s, the high fashion styles of the Parisian *haute couture* industry reached extremes of design to the point of ludicrous garment styles. The ready-to-wear industry capitalised on the practical styles they offered and the fact that the quality of their garments was by this time very much higher. This, coupled with the relaxation of status and class division, assisted the growth of the ready-to-wear industry, even though the ability to meet the demands of the mass market was still somewhat hit and miss.

Early twentieth century designers

More designers opened their houses during the early years of the twentieth century, including Paul Poiret in 1903 and Coco Chanel in 1915. These two designers were much copied and succeeded in making their designs accessible to more than just the wealthy upper classes. Chanel demonstrated her business talents by using synthetic fibres within her couture designs, making them more affordable to a wider audience without discrediting her design talent. World War I interrupted fashion and its associated industries from 1914 to 1918.

The Color Association of the United States

In 1915, The Color Association of the United States (CAUS) became involved in colour forecasting. The ready-to-wear industry had established itself in America much earlier than in Britain. Although it was possible to copy the styles of Paris relatively quickly, there was a growing need to provide more insight into colour direction at an earlier stage in order for the fibre, yarn and fabric manufacturers to be prepared for the requirements of the garment manufacturers.

Post-war influences

The end of World War I brought much celebration. The behaviour of women changed considerably since they had gained their freedom and independence, which by now was socially acceptable. Women worked in jobs previously held by men during the war effort. By 1918 they had won the right to vote in Britain, and in the USA by 1920. Many new influences became important – dancing, music, sports and hobbies. Art crazes such as Op Art, Art Deco and Art Nouveau were popular at this time and the latter brought art products to the lower classes. Theatre also became popular and costume designers were much copied by fashion designers, such as Bakst's designs for Diaghilev's Ballets Russes, copied by Paul Poiret. Inspiration for fashion design at this time was taken from almost anything.

The 1920s

Research in the man-made fibre industry began to increase rapidly and production methods were further developed to attain higher speeds, more varied yarns and fabrics, and a higher end-product quality. The most problematic aspect for the ready-to-wear industry in Britain seemed to be garment fit. It was in this area that *haute couture* had excelled. Garments were made to fit the individual client. The present day standard sizing system was not adopted from the USA until much later. However, the loose, straight silhouette of the 1920s eliminated many of the problems of fit and the ready-to-wear industry was able to establish itself easily, offering completely made garments, 'off the peg', giving an acceptable fit for many, thanks to the style of the era. This enabled the introduction of a new marketing approach – the boutique – a concept that the department stores were to later adopt. Though at this time, many dressmakers were still providing a service making fitted garments for individual clients.

As cheap fabrics became more readily available along with easy-to-follow paper patterns, the establishment of the second-hand clothing trade and cheaper ready-to-wear garments contributed to making fashion more easily accessible to all classes. Also, by this time, the middle and lower classes were increasingly better off and women were being educated at colleges and universities, which was instrumental in women attaining better paid jobs.

The American influence

By the 1920s, New York had established itself as a fashion city. Travel was becoming easier and cheaper, allowing manufacturers to go abroad for inspiration and knowledge of fashion direction. Entertainment was also becoming big business and with the development of Hollywood, the cinema became an important place for the general public to frequent. Thus, actresses became excellent promoters of fashion, displaying styles, colours and images to all.

Early consumer demand

By the mid 1920s, the younger generation became significant directors of lifestyle and fashion. Cheaper colour production in printing made magazines more popular. Accurate colour and details were necessary to replicate the precise look. As women increasingly displayed their own freedom and individuality, consumer demand was beginning to be felt by the fashion and textile industry.

Paris couturiers were now starting to see their leadership threatened, and bespoke garments became less profitable and less important. Many houses realised that their business outlook had to change if they were to survive and with this, their design ideas now became more marketable than their bespoke garments.

Tobe Associates and The Fashion Group

In 1927, Tobe Coller Davis established Tobe Associates consultancy in the USA. While it is not certain that this was the first consultancy of its kind, it was undoubtedly the most important one at the time. At last a company existed that could concentrate on the fundamentals of fashion direction to be delivered to the manufacturers in exchange for a fee, freeing the manufacturers of this process and allowing them to concentrate their efforts on production. Obviously, as many manufacturers were supplied with the same information, a theme was set and followed by the subscribers of the company. If a theme is promoted widely and made readily available, then more successful sales will follow, principally, as the population recognises it as the 'in look'. Tobe Associates' business increased in both capacity and importance during the 1930s.

In 1928 another important fashion concept was formulated in the USA – The Fashion Group – which eventually came into being in 1931 by founder members including Edna Woolman Chase, Claire McCardell and Elizabeth Arden. The publication of fashion trend reports was an important aspect of this organisation. Records from its establishment in 1931 to the present day are held in its own archive at the original headquarters in the Rockefeller Center, New York.

The 1930s

By the 1930s, there had been much development in the knit-wear industry, enabling the production of high quality fabrics at increased production speeds. Designer Elsa Schiaparelli often used knitted fabrics in her designs and this helped to upgrade the image of knitwear. The ready-to-wear sector of the industry was by now well established and the man-made fibre industry was developing new synthetic fibres, such as nylon, produced in abundance in the USA in 1938.

Retail

By the 1930s, the boutique had become a very influential vehicle for fashion marketing. It became evident that mass production needed mass marketing techniques in order to keep ahead of the increasing competition. Branding and particularly brand names also became a very important marketing technique at this time, which has now become an integral part of the marketing philosophy. Brand names and brand identity are important measures of customer recognition. Berkertex, originally established in 1910 became one of the most influential brands of the 1930s, as well as Windmoor and Alexon. The concept of branding was identified and much expanded upon by Marks & Spencer who, in 1930, adopted the use of their own label, 'St Michael'. A few years later, Marks & Spencer established their development department and in 1936, a design department, in order to take full control of not only the retail aspects of the business, but also the product range development, thereby becoming predominantly a marketing-led department store.

The need for fashion forecasting

Haute couture fashions had now became much more out-rageous, possibly to distinguish them from the ready-to-wear fashions that were more practical in style, meeting the demands of the poorer classes. However, it would appear that the less frivolous women were looking for more practical styles and designs that better reflected their moods, differing social behaviour and leisure pursuits. As *haute couture* began to lose its dominance as a driving force of fashion, the need to forecast consumer demand for the ready-to-wear industry became more evident.

The ready-to-wear industry was increasing in popularity and large department stores began to employ fashion buyers. The fashion buyer is now, and was then, responsible for making final decisions on the products the store will stock, including aspects related to quality specifications and pricing policies. Buyers are also now expected to present trends, both visually through mood boards (discussed in Chapter 6) and verbally to co-workers in the company's marketing department. Buyers therefore need insight into the demands of the consumer and also knowledge of likely future fashion trends. The buyers' role probably became a necessity within both the retail and manufacturing sectors as a direct result of the increased rate of change and direction of fashion change during this and subsequent decades of the twentieth century.

The British Colour Council

In 1931 The British Colour Council (BCC) was formed and played a key role in the forecasting of seasonal colour palettes. Their information was presented to fibre, yarn and fabric manufacturers in advance of the appropriate season. At this time, the responsibility for colour direction was still very much with the manufacturers. The communication gap between the consumer and the manufacturer increased due to the manufacturer not having a one-to-one relationship with the consumer, as did the bespoke designers with their clients. As a result, it became more difficult for manufacturers to understand consumers' needs in what was becoming an increasingly competitive economic climate. It became apparent that to survive within the industry, manufacturers needed to be able to accurately predict or anticipate consumer demand.

Garment sizing and fit

The fashions of the 1930s became more stylised and fitted. As ready-to-wear garments were intended to fit women of all sizes and figure types, the figure-fitting styles were problematic for the British ready-to-wear industry, as unlike in

America at this time, a standard sizing system had not yet been developed in Britain. While the use of shoulder pads promoted in couture designs did relieve some of the problems encountered with fit, many problems still remained by the end of this decade.

The size designation system for the British garment manufacturing industry was introduced in the early 1940s. Sizes are based on the average figure type and proportions, and are used uniformly by the garment manufacturing industry for the basic blocks from which completed designs are developed. These are body measurements not garment measurements, the designer decides how much 'ease' (extra fabric) to add to the garment for movement and style, therefore two size 12 dresses of different design will not necessarily have the same circumference measurements.

Figure types depend upon proportion in terms of the length of the torso, the position of the bust point, hip circumference in relationship to waist measurement, and the difference between the bust, waist and hip measurements. Other considerations are given to the averages of height, neck and wrist circumferences, and shoulder drop. The standard body measurements therefore include the bust, waist and hip measurement; back waist length (taken from the base of the neck to the waistline); sleeve length from the shoulder to the wrist; arm circumference (taken 2.5 cm below the armpit); and dress/skirt length measured from the waistline to mid-knee. As it is the average sizes and figure type on which the standard sizing and grading system is based, a perfect fit will not be achievable for every women. However, the designer will aim at what would hopefully be considered an acceptable fit for the consumer. Standard sizing systems not only assist the manufacturer in producing acceptably fitting garments for the consumer, but also help the consumer purchase clothing without having to try on many garments to find those that fit.

Other influences

In 1937 Carlin International was established, offering manufacturers an alternative source of forecasting information. By the end of this decade the British fashion industry was threatened by the onset of World War II (1939–1945). The effect of war restricted the industry's output throughout the next decade. Uniforms and work wear took precedence over fashion, and fabrics were rationed. Due to high audience numbers, cinema became the focal point not just for entertainment purposes but also for the dissemination of news, making it an ideal marketing vehicle for advertising new fashion styles.

The 1940s

The 1940s became very much a 'make do and mend' era as manufacturers were restricted in the amount of fabric used in designs. Styles were also restricted due to ethical issues of a country at war; it was considered inappropriate to be highly stylish. However, while the availability of new fabrics and garments was tightly controlled, women were using their dressmaking and hand-knitting skills along with their own design ideas to produce their own individual look. Old clothes were up-dated with new buttons and trims and wealthier women paid seamstresses to make new garments from their husbands' suits while they were at war. The need to look and feel womanly in an otherwise male dominated and unsettled period became the driving force of style at a time of war and economic deprivation.

The fashion industry

In 1944 The Fashion Institute of Technology was formed to support the New York fashion industry. In 1945 Parisian couture was re-established. Pierre Balmain and Hardy Amies among others opened their houses. Frederick Starke showed the first wholesale collection in couture style. This had a great influence on the status of the ready-to-wear industry. Development in the synthetic fibre industry was stimulated by the war, as it was difficult to obtain imported natural fibres.

Post-war

Important developments in the man-made fibre and yarn industry accelerated after the war and Dior promoted his 'New Look', a term coined by Mrs Carmel Snow, fashion editor of *Harper's Bazaar*. Dior originally called this new look 'corolla' as the wearer appears to emerge from the middle of opening petals; the highly flared and stiffened skirt. The bodice of the new look emphasised femininity with soft rounded shoulders and none of the heavy shoulder-pads of pre-war styles. Attention was given to the very slim waistline which was further accentuated by the 'ballet tutu' style of the skirt with a hemline of approximately 10 cm below the knee, and even lower in subsequent seasons. In 1947 the Royal College of Art opened its fashion school, which was responsible for producing many of the designers of the latter part of this century. The American standard sizing system began to be employed by British manufacturers and designers improving the fit of ready-to-wear garments. By the end of the 1940s, Balmain had opened his boutique and many other couture designers were producing ready-to-wear or prêt-à-porter collections.

The London Model House Group was formed in 1947 by a group of manufacturers. It began to co-ordinate a structure for the industry by introducing seasonal stock to the retailing sector. It was responsible for adjusting the timing of fashion shows to more manageable time-scales of production and promotion within the retail season calendar. This helped the manufacturer work to deadlines on the heavier weight clothing now associated with the autumn/winter season, and on the lighter weight garments of the spring/summer season. This system is still in use today, though with the changing climate in Britain, the timing of stock change-over in stores may benefit from a further restructure.

The 1950s

During the 1950s there were technical developments in spinning techniques and synthetic fibres/yarn developments including Du Pont's Orlon which was in full production by the early 1950s, and Dacron in 1951. ICI established Terylene in 1952 and the same year Chemstrand Corporation developed Acrilian. Acrylic yarn production was by now a major competitor to the wool industry – a threat from which it never recovered. Loom technology boosted the production of woven fabric manufacturers, and greater speeds on circular knitting machines and warp knitting machines were evident in the growing knitting industry. Higher sewing machine speeds also assisted the garment manufacturing industry, rapidly increasing production.

Other technology in this sector of the industry included Singer's tacking and button machines; laser cutters; computerised sewing machines; and the development of the safety stitch by the Union Machine Company which was very important in ensuring quality in ready-to-wear clothing, as it prevented seams undoing. By now colours and fabrics were establishing a more seasonal direction on the high street, as a direct result of forecasting and promoting new seasonal colours through exhibitions such as Interstoff. This major textile show established in Germany in 1959 to promote fabrics, offering support to the textile manufacturing industry as well as inspiration to the garment production sector. Paris and Milan were both now important cities for British and American manufacturers to visit for inspiration.

Driving forces

The younger generation was beginning to enjoy increased spending power as the economy began to recover after the war years; fashion became an ideal commodity for their freedom of expression and individuality and the fashion industry began to focus strongly on this market. Hence, fashion became more directed towards the younger generation. With more women in employment, easy-care fabrics and fibres became of prime importance. Many tactics were developed by manufacturers to promote their advantages to the consumer. By now the social revolution had taken place. The poor were less poor and the wealthy were becoming a less elite class as more business entrepreneurs joined the higher earning bracket.

In 1954 Chanel re-opened her house after closing in 1939 at the outbreak of war, and aggressively promoted her style in what was still a predominantly male environment. The following year another important female designer of the twentieth century, Mary Quant, opened her first boutique in London. At this time, Parisian couturiers were closely watching the directions of the American ready-to-wear industry, which was influencing the prêt-à-porter collections. This highlights a turning point in the fashion as the importance of ready-to-wear overtook that of bespoke clothing.

By the end of the 1950s, music had increased its importance in popular entertainment and in turn began to influence fashion, in particular Rock 'n' Roll and the 'Teddy Boy' look for the males and the 'Tutu' style skirts for the females. In 1959 the Barbie doll was marketed as the first adult-looking doll. Its fashionable wardrobe promoted the concept of fashion to an even younger generation.

The need for forecasting

A fashion disaster occurred in the late 1960s and early 1970s when the midi skirt was introduced. This was the result of manufacturers failing to read or anticipate consumer demand correctly on the timing of acceptability to changing the hem-line. The result of this misinterpretation led to serious financial loss and business closures. While not the first costly fashion flop of this century, it was certainly the most devastating to the industry and highlighted the need for more accurate fashion direction prediction to prevent this kind of mistake from happening again.

During the 1960s more colour and fashion consultancy businesses were established, including Informa Inc. and Promostyl. Others included International Colour Association (ICA) who uniquely predicted trends 18 months in advance.

The 1970s

In the early 1970s fashion lacked direction and no single influential driving force could be identified. Music became more varied as did the style of its associated clothing. Consumer demand in turn became more varied which influenced the need for market segmentation in retailing. The many fashion consultancies now in operation seemed to lack a common theme for any particular season. No longer could designers or manufacturers dictate to the consumer and forecasting their demands now became a vital factor for the industry.

As well as the problems of the fashion and associated industries, Britain's industries in general – but particularly the heavy industries – were hit by economic recession. Consumer spending once again became restricted, though some support was available through state benefits.

Despite the recession, many known and unknown designers opened houses and boutiques, though the emphasis was on ready-to-wear. Fashion retailing became large-scale and lost the intimacy of the boutique. This exacerbated the effects of the lack of direction in fashion. Still more forecasting companies became established, including Design Intelligence and the British Textile Colour Group (BTCG), possibly in an attempt to re-direct fashion in an otherwise receding industry. Also, the service industry sector was now offering new business opportunities, due to the low set-up costs compared to those in manufacturing. Many skilled personnel had lost their manufacturing jobs in the factories that had been victims of the recession and poor business management; these people were in a good position, with their knowledge of the industry, to set themselves up in this new service sector.

The retailing concept of Next

By the end of the 1970s, Next hit the high street with their new concept of retailing. They used a limited colour palette per season and exploited display methods for optimum sales as their key marketing strategy. This emphasised the effective use of colour in fashion retailing, echoing the thinking of the initial colour forecasting companies and exhibition directors that had occurred 40 years previously.

The 1980s

As Britain began to recover from the recession, computer technology became increasingly utilised in fibre, yarn, fabric and garment production. *Haute couture* lost its role as a driving force of fashion, as many sources of inspiration became acceptable, making fashion styling more varied, mirroring the changing lifestyles of consumers. Consumers became more individual as many different leisure pursuits were available to them. Sports and fitness became important and had a great impact upon casual fashions throughout the 1980s and

1990s. Television influenced the romantic styles promoted by period dramas and the high fashion styles promoted by American soap operas.

The establishment of the forecasting sector

More trade fairs were established during the 1980s, and although some consultancies such as Deryck Healey International ceased to trade, others such as Nelly Rodi forecasting services and Trend Union forecasting company were established. Competition between forecasting companies for business became evident. The need to survive in this growing sector was probably becoming a stronger driving force than the initial concept of an advisory service to the fashion and textile industry. The financial constraints of running a successful business may have affected the effectiveness of the forecasting process as companies concentrate on compiling trend prediction packages with a competitive edge, as opposed to the accuracy of the trend information meeting consumer demand and acceptability. The need for retailers to segment the market became ever more apparent due to a growing population with widely varying lifestyles and interests. Market research became an important tool for collating information about the consumer to assist retailers in targeting their market. This concept of identifying the lifestyle of the target market also became an important factor in the forecasting process.

The 1990s and the new millennium

Fashion retail sales figures of this final decade of the twentieth century show a steady decline in the industry, which has continued into the first four years of the new millenium. Again, no particular driving force could be identified for fashion direction. Much of the 1990s was dominated by the colour (or non-colour) grey as a staple. Grey is generally associated with non-movement, lack of motivation, stalemate; an accurate description of the effect it had upon high street sales.

The only glimmer of hope offered to the industry was the promise of the return of colour to the high street in the new millennium. This appeared to be implied by many trade magazines who promoted better utilisation of market segmentation by including consumer psychological data as well as demographic information. However, observing high street stores and the general public, as far into the new millenium as 2005, it would appear that colour is still struggling to be used to any great effect.

Summary

Inventions and developments in the fashion and textile industry over the past 300 years have been many and varied. As the industry grew in capacity and importance, and became capable of producing higher quality yarns, fabrics and end products quickly, so the demand from the consumer increased.

The earliest evidence of the need for forecasting was around 1825. However, it was a century later when the first forecasting company was established in the USA. During the 1930s similar companies were established in Britain. By the 1960s colour and fabrics had become more seasonal and more forecasting companies were established during the following two decades in Britain, the USA and in mainland Europe.

The consumer always has been, and always should be, considered as one of the major driving forces of fashion. In recent years, more money is spent on clothing as a desired commodity than as an absolute necessity. There are many more commodities and activities available, all competing for the consumer's disposable income.

Fashion has become a global phenomenon and with cheap and speedy import and export, the manufacturing of fashion is now globally competitive. Forecast companies sell their trend prediction packages throughout the world, offering a narrow palette to a wide captive audience. However, retailers have recognised the need to segment the market and source products specifically for their target customer. Forecasters have to seriously consider both market segmentation and product sourcing factors.

Marketing techniques and consumer research of desires rather than needs have become ever more important to the survival of the fashion and textile industry. This emphasises the fact that the current method of colour forecasting needs to be better understood to be used to its optimum capacity.

In this chapter

We have identified:

- the driving forces of fashion from the onset of the industrial revolution to present day
- the need for and the introduction of the forecasting sector.

In the next chapter we will evaluate the current body of knowledge in this specialist sector.

2

The views of forecasters and trend information users

The forecasting profession is seen as the backbone of the fashion and textile industry. We learnt in Chapter 1 how a specialist forecasting sector evolved to help relieve the manufacturers of this important task. However, designers and marketing professionals still take responsibility for forecasting their company's niche market using trend prediction packages as part of their source of inspiration. The colour forecasting process is thus not exclusive to the forecasting companies and key personnel in every manufacturing and retail business use variations of the same process.

We have already identified when, how and why the need for colour and fashion forecasting came about. We now look at what has been written to help us understand the forecasting process through what the forecasters do, how they do it and what they lead the world to believe about it. This will help us appreciate how the industry perceives the forecasting process and its effectiveness. We will discuss what colour forecasting is as well as its methodology.

The importance of colour forecasting

The products of the colour and trend forecasters are the trend packages they sell to the industry. The product of the fibre, yarn and fabric producers are the raw materials required by the garment manufacturers to produce garments for the retailers to sell to the consumers. The manufacturers' product is more important than the product of the colour forecasters and the latter is arguably dispensable without any detrimental effect on the industry, as long as the manufacturers take

In this chapter

We shall learn:

- the importance of colour forecasting for the fashion and textile industry
- the methodology of the colour forecasters
- further forecasting methods
- the skills involved in forecasting
- important aspects of colour and colour forecasting.

The main aim of this chapter is to introduce the language of forecasting and to discuss the process. Different view-points of both the process and its perceived importance in the industry are put forward by evaluating information and opinions available through printed media, conferences and discussions with design personnel.

control of the colour forecasting process. We have met many long-serving members of the manufacturing sector in the textile industry, who remember when their companies took responsibility for the colours made available to the 'downstream' sectors for forthcoming seasons.

While the forecasting profession was established as an independent sector to unburden manufacturers of the forecasting process, it can now be seen to monopolise the fashion and textile industry as the subscribers to the service lose control and foresight, creating uncertainty in trend direction and dependence upon the forecasters. The forecasters, in collaboration with the trade shows such as Expofil and Premier Vision, are promoting colour stories by creating a consensus (as discussed later). However, when a large majority of manufacturers follow this consensus, stores on the high street will lack variety for the consumer.

Forecasting and the promotion of trends could be seen as no more than a marketing technique to encourage sales on the high street by driving fashion through the use of seasonal colours. This would augment the importance of colour for the industry, and suggest that forecasting is an emotive aspect of marketing and a driving force of fashion.

On the other hand, forecasting can be construed as a hindrance to the industry's growth, by encouraging sales without any real improvement to quality. This may have encouraged price rivalry, replacing the style rivalry, potentially so detrimental to the fashion and textile industry. If the same fashion story is promoted world-wide, every manufacturer religiously uses the same information, inevitably producing similar products to sell globally. Style rivalry can not prevail as creativity is stifled and therefore price rivalry emerges, constricting the fashion and textile industry instead of stimulating it.

At present the accuracy of the forecasters inspires great confidence, whereas designers and marketing professionals appear less sure of their own judgements and feel safer following the promoted trends. Of course, the more they do this, the more likely the forecasts are to be accurate. However, this is simply manufacturers' accuracy in following trends, which does not necessarily create sales on the high street. The results of following trends rather than accurately forecasting the consumers' needs or desires, is reflected in the current high street sales figures and abundance of sales promotions.

The influence of the forecasters on the industry is thought by some to be highlighted by the power of promotion and advertising. The early colour groups such as the Color Association of the United States (CAUS) and the Colour Marketing Group (CMG) are made up of individuals who are in turn connected to the smaller colour forecasting services. Obviously they all promote the same colour stories after the initial colour palettes have been jointly approved. This validates the view of forecasting as self-fulfilling. However, it is important to acknowledge the significance of seasonal colour stories to the continuation of sales for the fashion and textile industry. It is not the process that is in question but rather the ability to anticipate consumer demand accurately.

As competitiveness in the fashion and textile industry has globalised, many manufacturers and retailers have tended to invest in trend prediction information, simply to survive. However, rather than staying one step ahead of the competitors, everyone seems to be working with the same information, producing similar results.

The real significance of colour forecasting for the industry emerged in response to the lack of direction or colour co-ordination during the 1970s, when the industry was heavily promoting mix-and-match separates to assist the consumer during the economic recession. However, with shop layouts resembling jumble sales, the industry needed even more help. Retailing became more focused during the 1980s as the retailing company Next embarked on its colour co-ordinating marketing strategy and through the introduction of target marketing. Colour forecasting became an influential tool for assessing the direction of colour and its rate of change, rather than predicting specific colours to be reproduced.

The information user must be creative in the application of the trend predictions, in order to offer the consumer something different. However, the uncertainty felt by the industry did not encourage such an approach. Whether or not forecasting and trend promotion are seen as a conspiracy, their impact on the fashion and textile industry cannot be denied.

Colour forecasting methodology

Many fashion authors have outlined the basic forecasting methodology but the process has never been explained in depth. While methods differ slightly between forecasters, all aim at predicting what the consumer desires by evaluating their moods and observing their behaviour.

Trade magazines have sometimes reported accounts of the colour selection process, from the initial colour meetings to the retailers, though no attempt has been made to describe the methodology of each stage of the process. In essence, when compiling a colour range there is generally a set criteria for the number of colours, the colour combinations and illustrations used to convey the story, as set out by the company. Brainstorming sessions are an integral part of the process and the aim is to identify and follow the natural evolution of fashion for the forecasts. Evidence of exactly how this is achieved, however, has not been recorded.

Forecasters appreciate the evolutionary nature of colours and predict future preferences based upon a natural transition, i.e. evolution. Transition is used here to mean change of direction; evolution is used to convey change over time. These two concepts – direction of change and rate of change – are important tools used by the forecaster in the colour forecasting process. Identifying colour movement and rate of colour change from season to season assists the fibre, yarn and fabric manufacturers to establish an effective approach to colour forecasting for themselves.

As we do not replace the entire contents of our wardrobes every season, the next season's colours need to harmonise with those of the previous one, otherwise we would never buy anything new because we had nothing to mix and match it with. From a commercial point of view, colours need to change radically enough to add freshness to the new season's garments and create sales but slowly enough to allow for affordable replenishment of the wardrobe. The colour forecaster must be aware of the consumers' acceptability of the direction of change and the acceptable timing of this change. A system that works in conjunction with sales data can provide a valuable colour forecasting tool but the consumers' demands and desires must be anticipated accurately and met. Some see the role of the colour forecaster as demonstrating new colour ways but not enforcing them on the general public. The industry, however, would still need more accurate forecasts than mere colour promotions. The notion of forecaster as 'demonstrator' is no more than a get-out clause for poor forecasting.

Li Edelkoort, founder of Trend Union, describes data collection for forecasting as an ongoing process. The forecaster then intuitively selects colours from this source of inspiration and Edelkoort perceives this step as a crucial stage of the forecasting process. However, this intuition is never questioned or exposed to more critical reasoning so the methodology remains shrouded in mystery and a monopoly is created for forecasters.

Edelkoort promotes the idea that forecasting methodology is artistic in nature and that it is not possible to apply any objective investigation. She also credits merchandisers and buyers with employing the same intuitive methodology when buying stock, claiming that personal tastes bear no influence. There is however evidence suggesting that forecasting does not require this gift of intuition and is in fact more systematic. This makes the application a scientific methodology for repeated use by the novice a possibility, thus enabling newcomers to the field to be trained in a systematic way.

Julie Buddy, a colour and fashion consultant for Informada, London (a fashion consultancy established in 1965) has been involved in the colour consultancy profession for over 40 years, working with many of the major fibre companies and retailers. She identified three main areas in the colour forecasting process: exploration; evaluation and analysis; and collation of all the information into a fashion marketing concept. She views market research as a fundamental tool for the forecaster enabling the process of observation to be consistent. Consumer segmentation was also pinpointed by Buddy as an essential tool.

A further approach recognises the importance of forecasting to the industry but views colour forecasting as purely objective with intuition playing no part in the process, thus enabling fashion prediction to be recorded and logically explained. Others conversely claim that the skill of forecasting involves a sixth sense.

One can justifiably question whether or not the forecasters consciously conspire to protect their monopoly over the industry or whether they simply do not accept that their methodology can be recorded and used in a systematic manner. Whatever the truth, it is clear that the industry recognises the need for a better method for this all important market sector.

The forecasting process explained

At a conference in Glasgow in 1999, Li Edelkoort gave the following brief account of the methodology used by the forecaster. Colour representations of interest, which appeal, or for any other reason known only to the individual, are collected on an ongoing basis throughout the year in any form or substance, be it sweet papers, stones or fabric. These samples are stored in drawers according to their hue. Every six months, when the time comes to put together a new colour palette, colour representations are selected from the drawers in an intuitive way. Edelkoort claims that she takes out of the drawer those colours which are most appealing to the eye. Many colours are selected in this way and laid out on a surface. Natural colour stories, she says, are then identified from the array of colour representations. Edelkoort's reports of how she views and carries out these processes are always very vague, offering no real insight into her methodology. Ideas for fashion begin to formulate around the colours and are then developed into story boards which are shown at colour meetings. Again, exactly how these ideas are formulated is never divulged, keeping the process mystical and secret.

Everyone at the colour meetings (including fibre manufacturers, designers and forecasters) bring along their colour story boards developed in much the same manner. Similarities are drawn considering both the inspiration behind the colour stories and any word associations, as well as the actual colours themselves. Discussions are then held and eventually a colour palette is agreed. There is no explanation of how these meetings are organised, who is allowed to attend, or who authorises current or future participants.

Many authors have come to the conclusion that the similarities in forecasts exist simply because everyone involved is viewing the world from the same angle, reading the same signs, using the same inspirational sources.

Tim Hulse researched and reported on the British Textile Colour Group in 1999, speaking to its founder member, Joanna Bowering who describes how a panel of 25 bring together their own colour stories in the form of storyboards to the meeting. Each presents their boards, conveying the moods and colours and reasoning they anticipate for the next season. By explaining the reasoning behind their choices they establish the concept of their colour stories in the minds of these present. A consensus is formed on similarities of images, words, moods and colours and by the end of the meeting a colour card has been agreed. The card is then taken to a meeting at Intercolor, Paris, an independent group of about 25 members from all over the world who meet to decide on colours for women's wear by repeating the process again, showing their country's colour stories. The resulting colour card is then available to purchase by the fibre, yarn and fabric manufacturers for their interpretations. Premier Vision (PV) is a three day show for the fabric manufacturers to exhibit their current and new fabric ranges. Its importance has become well known as the 'colour filter' for the industry, largely due to the exhibition compiling its own colour card, in which Edelkoort plays a part. Those exhibiting at PV will also use PV's own colour card, as only fabrics containing their colour selection will be exhibited. It is the strength and certainty of the colour presentations at the exhibitions that instills confidence in the buyers when they attend the different trade shows.

Some forecasters such as Joanna Bowering believe colour forecasting to be a decision-making process; some believe it to be one of intuition; and some have been reported to confess to the whole thing being entirely made up. These differing viewpoints on how the forecasting process works in reality can be considered to fuel the argument of a monopoly protected by secrecy. On the other hand, there are masters and cowboys in every trade: some could be working with the utmost integrity and best intentions to produce accurate forecasts; while others may compile anything for profit.

The role of trade exhibitions

Premier Vision is recognised as one of the most popular and important exhibitions as a source of inspiration. It is therefore easy to understand why this exhibition is the focus of the industry, acting as a colour filter. The exhibition begins with the meeting of the panel members at the PV office. The panel consists of at least 80 members from all areas of the fashion industry. It works on the colour ranges 18 months ahead of the season in question. Meetings are held for members to discuss the season, the market and to select a colour range. The colours are then grouped into themes and market sectors.

Further discussions are held to refine the colours into an acceptable shade card, though we were unable to identify specific information on the number of colours selected, nor any further indications of how the colours are selected, or to uncover where the inspirations come from.

Meetings are then arranged in France, Spain, Italy, Belgium and Great Britain, presenting the colour ranges to the fibre, yarn and fabric companies. One month before Premier Vision, the Paris office receives weavers' fabrics for display. Each fabric sample is checked against the PV colour shade card and the samples containing colours not represented on the colour card are rejected. This ensures that the whole exhibition relates to the colour stories set by the panel for that season, instilling and promoting a consensual theme.

Successful fabrics are used for display, the fabric resource library and samples of each are sent to Li Edelkoort at Trend Union for the assembly of her audio-visual presentation. Her team collates samples of the same colour to present as the strong colour story. The rest of the colours are promoted as the fashion or accent colours. Around 450 trend boards are made for the exhibition, supported by a wealth of accessory props to help communicate the mood and to accentuate the colour stories.

Trade shows and exhibitions are required to use set criteria and this ensures that everyone exhibiting conforms to a trend supported by the exhibition's own prediction package. Buyers will pick up this continuity of colour and read it as the trend colours. They include some or all of the colours in their selections and so emphasise the trend and collectively deliver it to the high street where it is assumed that consumers will recognise the colour story being promoted to them. As a result, predicted colours therefore become the reality.

The colour story promotion tactics of the organisers of Premier Vision state that 12 shades are to be promoted by the exhibitions' own trend packages. It is compulsory for exhibitors to include these colours in their own ranges.

Subjectivity and objectivity

Colour forecasting has two basic aspects: a scientific and objective one; and a more subjective, and less tangible one. Colour can be measured accurately using technology – from simple devices such as colorimeters to more sophisticated apparatus such as spectrophotometers. Alternatively, colour can be discussed in a looser way, using less clearly defined terminology. At present, the latter approach prevails, possibly due to the lack of published research. The most important aspects of colour forecasting have been identified as anticipating the correct timing of change; the direction that the change takes; and how consumers react to the change. Most agree that there is a mix of both art and science involved in the process. Art in the high input of judgement, intuition and knowledge stored in the conscious and subconscious mind; and science in the more analytical processes. However, forecasters would prefer the forecasting process to be seen as strictly an art – even a gift – so that they can retain a monopoly over the process.

The ideal methodology should include a combination of tools from both the artistic and scientific approaches. These tools, as well as the general forecasting methods available and those used specifically by fashion forecasters, are discussed and evaluated in the following pages.

With forecasters undoubtedly promoting the belief that their art is an acquired one, they are in effect discouraging the development of a methodology for colour forecasting for the fibre, yarn and fabric manufacturing industry to use.

Forecasting skills

The three skills that the forecaster needs to develop for the process of colour forecasting are awareness, observation and intuition. These are predominantly subjective or art-based skills. The more tangible skills include analysis, evaluation and data interpretation.

Awareness

Awareness is a highly personal but important aspect, continual throughout the forecasting process. Patterns are memorised from a number of sources, including people observed on the streets and in shops, old clothing trends, socio-political developments and financial cycles. This information is collected visually and stored in the memory, to be later analysed and refined into trends. It is a systematic approach but one which remains unrecorded and therefore unavailable for use by others.

Observation skills

Intuition can be developed through observation which continually absorbs information from our surroundings. This is a precursor to the awareness process. First we see the things around us – very much a subconscious act; and it is only once we become aware of the information we have taken in that the data is brought into our consciousness. The forecaster is trained to become more aware of what is observed and this in turn makes more conscious use of observation. When first selecting colours, memory takes an active part in the process. As more of the same colour is observed, the memory activates the recognition of patterns observed recently in the environment and this information is brought into the conscious mind, making the forecaster aware of the patterns. Awareness and observation clearly go hand in hand but because the data they generate is rarely recorded, it remains subjective and its accuracy cannot be challenged. There is also the problem of colour memory and how accurately a particular colour can be recalled; this is discussed on p. 41.

Intuition

Many are adamant that intuition is the key to successful colour forecasting and see it as the most important tool. Intuition is particularly significant when the forecaster comes to the stage in the process where all the information is brought together into presentable and convincing colour stories. Colour plays a pivotal role in the fashion business; the industry believes that once the colour aspect of design is right, then all else will fall into place. Companies are therefore willing to invest large amounts of money in forecasters, in the hope that their business will survive. These companies are investing heavily in other people's intuition but the information users (i.e. their designers and buyers) are then expected to use their intuition to select the best colours from the range for their company's use. If the forecasting process was better understood by the industry, subscription fees could be saved and a more diverse selection of garments would be available on the high street, encouraging style rivalry once more instead of price rivalry.

Sourcing and collecting information

There are many avenues available for sourcing information for the development of predictive colour and style stories for a company's new season collection. However, the reasoning behind colour selection is not evident due to the lack of current research in this area.

Methods of forecasting

Both general and specific forecasting methods are used by the colour and fashion forecaster. The general forecasting ones are those with a scientific basis which can be recorded and analysed. These include researching the economy, demographics, technical developments and socio-cultural trends. These aspects have different value for each forecasting sector. Demographical trends are of little consequence to the initial colour forecasters predicting for a diverse clientele, e.g. the apparel and the home furnishings industries. Demographic trends however, are generally important to market sectors such as women's knitwear manufacturers.

During recessions, fashion becomes less prominent and classical styles and colours are more likely to be popular, whereas during periods of affluence, novelty is more likely to be accepted. This clearly has a great effect on the acceptability and changing proportions of staple and fashion colours, particularly fad colours. Similarly, technical developments such as dyeing techniques may provide impetus for new colours, perhaps specific to certain fibres. The fibre and yarn producers have a vested interest in these particular shades being popularised. Consumer demand is affected by various factors, including changes in the national economy, demographic trends, technical developments and the socio-cultural environment (lifestyles).

Fashion-specific forecasting methods

Fashion-specific forecasting methods include both artistic and scientific approaches. The process of taking historical data, linked with the controversial use of cycles is an important, though less accepted, method of fashion and colour forecasting. The debate about colour cycles arises from different viewpoints. Some recognise cycles in the tonal values of colours popular throughout history, while others argue that the actual colours are cyclic. Most are in agreement that colours come into fashion and then go out of fashion, though no real evidence of timing of this can be identified. A systematic approach to analysing the changes of colour in forecasts and the level of acceptability by the consumer may be too large a task to be undertaken by forecasters. Few companies would be willing to fund this type of extensive research. Only if initial findings indicated that colour precision was of significant importance to the consumer could such research be justified.

Fashion-specific forecasting methods could usefully study the last five to ten years to assist forecasting trends for the immediate future. Cycles can be seen as more systematic for long-run trends but not for the short-run trends, known as fads. Further research is necessary to validate this view.

Other fashion-specific forecasting methods include the measurement of the diffusion of fashion, employing diffusion curves developed using the number of adopters over points of time. The rate and current level of acceptance are analysed and it is possible to estimate the extent of the trend. Current levels of acceptance is something forecasters observe, whether or not they are conscious of the fact; they prefer to view this activity as part of their intuition.

Consumer surveys, consumer panels and test marketing, as well as the monitoring of designer collections, fashion cities and the high street are all sources of data considered to be fashion-specific.

Other specific forecasting approaches

Other scientific approaches include data collection from consumer surveys and panels, market testing, analysing sales trends, and consumer spending habits. In order to measure the diffusion of colour, a database of historical information is required. Qualitative and quantitative forecasting methods offer a more valuable method of forecasting and both long and short-range techniques are generally needed. Predictions can then be tailored to the specific consumer segment.

Quantitative methods measure in units which can be interpreted scientifically via sales figures to indicate consumer acceptability. Quantitative methods have been developed for consumer behaviour analysis, though not for fashion prediction; this could be further investigated. Marketing techniques in the fashion sector have advanced significantly in the last decades of the century and the analysis of consumer behaviour is widely accepted as an important aspect of forecasting as the concept of lifestyles has progressively become more integral to the process.

Qualitative methods take a subjective assessment and generally are used in the form of observation skills by fashion forecasters. Observation here is the use of the eyes and ears. However, the lack of a precise verbal colour system leaves this method somewhat fallible and knowledge of the levels of colour accuracy and acceptability become of paramount importance.

Long and short range forecasting methods

There are two types of forecasting – short range and long range. The main difference between them is the time-scale involved and their accuracy. Short range is more accurate due to its shorter time span, from a few months up to two years. Long range forecasts covering three to five years have a higher risk of inaccuracy due to unforeseen events. Short range forecasts are therefore more appropriate for forecasting fashion. Trends are identified and the levels of demand for them assessed, as well as the timing of acceptability by the consumer. Long range forecasts are more appropriate for planning marketing strategies.

The time required by the industry to produce garments and sell them to the retailers means that the forecasters work about two years ahead. As the industry is now experiencing demands of quick response from the retailers, producing orders on demand, those manufacturers using their own forecasting process would benefit from reduced time-scales.

Interpretation of information

Methods of evaluation and interpretation of information as well as the presentation of data are discussed by many authors and depend for the most part on staff of the retail companies, though advice is sometimes taken from fashion consultancies. However, the thought processes of these activities are at best briefly described and little understood.

Interpretation requires a preliminary process of eliminating any information not considered to be applicable to the season or to the company profile. This elimination may be based on intuition or on a more objective approach. The data that remains forms the colour story to be presented to the company's staff. The presenter of the information has to be skilled in putting across with conviction a credible story; confidence and persuasion are necessary to communicate the right mood.

Key aspects of colour forecasting

Colour cycles

Colour cycles are patterns with fixed or regular occurrences. Some writers argue that no fixed or regularly recurring cycles have been identified in fashion. Two aspects of colour cycles that are widely recognised, however, are movement of colour preference and repetition of popularity of specific colours. It has been suggested that the driving force for the former is boredom. But how do the forecasts compare with the popular colours that were actually worn at the time and do these colour cycles still apply today?

Researchers have found evidence of swings from high chroma (bright) colours to multi-coloured, to subdued, to earth tones, to achromatics, to purple phases and back to high chroma colours. As much as a seven-year period has been identified between cool and warm tones. Cycles can be based upon hue, intensity and colour 'temperature'.

There is little evidence of analysis of the movement and repetitiveness of colour over time and few investigations of this nature have been conducted in academia. Although the life cycles of fashions are a potentially useful tool for the forecaster, there is still no clear methodology recorded for the movement of fashion colours in order to understand the colour forecasting process.

In the past, colour was used as a back-drop to style, whereas today, it is becoming more of a driving force of fashion and fashion purchases. Rigorous research would be needed to corroborate this claim. Interestingly, it is colour moods rather than the individual colours which are considered to move in cycles.

Colour cycles are referred to as revivals, where past fashions inspire new styles. Cycles are seen in an inspirational context and not as a rigid pattern. Therefore a prediction methodology can not be linked directly to fashion history, though some argue that patterns are marked enough to validate the importance of fashion history as a predictive source. Some forecasters believe that colour patterns are indeed cyclic in the sense of being in and out of fashion, though no formula exists to express rate or direction of change.

Staple colours and fashion colours

Forecasters refer to staple colours, which are considered to be the 'bread and butter' colours for the industry and which have a relatively long shelf-life, e.g. black and navy. Fashion colours or fad colours come and go more quickly, possibly in fashion for just one season, e.g. purple and lime. Staple colours are often used by the forecasters and by designers to 'anchor' fashionable colours. Reports of fashion trends have been misleading in the past, assuming that colour cycles are a ploy by the industry to profit by focusing on specific colours instead of trying to offer a wider colour range to the consumer. While it would make economic sense for the industry to operate in this manner, in reality the change of colour from season to season would be too quick for the retailers to benefit. Colours often referred to historically as cyclic fashion colours have become generally adopted now by the colour forecasting industry as staple ones, i.e. dark blues, greens, browns and greys, beige, black and white. Research into the rate of change of staple and fashion colours would be valuable.

Colour precision and colour communication

There is some doubt about the accuracy of colours promoted by the colour and fashion prediction services, when in-depth information is reported to clients as quickly as one week after attending a trade exhibition. Although fashion styles and details can be accurately interpreted in a relatively short space of time, it is doubtful that colour can be accurately reproduced as quickly.

There is no evidence of precise methods for colour measurement by trend reporters, nor of the accuracy of the colour information reported back to the design office. So it is not clear how close the reproduced colours in the final trend packages are to the original inspiration at trade exhibitions, nor any suggestions as to how accurate this needs to be. As hand-held colour measurement systems are becoming more widely available this problem could be partially alleviated, though the accuracy of reproducing colours may still be in question. We have occasionally found discrepancies in colours within a single prediction package; for example, a colour of specified name and number has varied in tonal value on different pages of the package.

Colour names, semantics and communication

While the generic name of a colour gives some indication of a hue's intensity and value, it does not convey the precise colour in one's mind. If personnel verbally communicate their observations from trade fairs back to the designers in the office, drastic colour differences will occur. While some colour references exist – two examples being CAUS standard colour reference of America, and Pantone – how widely these or any similar systems are used is not known.

Forecasters believe that colour names are beginning to develop significance in forecasting. Some working in the science of colour perception argue that humans develop colour perception over generations. Colour names are used as a marketing tool with names given to represent a mood or renew an otherwise dated colour. However, the language of colour is poorly communicated as not everyone's idea of a specifically named colour presents the exact same image of colour in mind. Creative people also tend to use their own versions of semantics, such as describing a colour as 'sexy', or 'zesty'. This language problem often creates barriers between the creative workers and those working more objectively. One can legitimately question how accurately the semantics used by colour reporters (e.g. for trade magazines) convey the colour story to the industry, and how precise this information needs to be.

Colour memory and communication of colour

Forecasters are renowned for keeping their methodology to themselves, relying on their memory. This is of no use to the researcher nor to newcomers to the profession. A more systematic approach is therefore beneficial. That is, a recorded system that identifies the process of change over time for future use. Until such a system exists, the forecasters will have a monopoly in the industry. Strong instinct can be developed over time, with appreciation and application of colour. Theoretically, almost anyone has the potential to be a colour forecaster, though the accuracy of trend predictions in relation to consumer desire or need remains the more important aspect of trend interpretation. There is a great need for a colour system to be used by forecasters which accurately matches colours from the initial source, unless that source is used only as inspiration, rather than the colour requirement.

Summary

There is an acceptance of the basic principles behind the process of colour forecasting, though the process has not yet been subjected to deeper investigation. The application of the forecasting process within the industry is variable and it is generally accepted that the process is both subjective (artistic) and objective (scientific). There is, however, still a need for a better understanding of the thought processes and decision-making involved, and what constitutes a good colour story or prediction.

The process of forecasting has become a more complex procedure over the last three decades as forecasters have realised the benefits of working more closely with, for example, sociologists and taking more account of consumer identification and consumer needs. This increased complexity has meant that many companies find it more cost effective to pay design consultants and forecasters to develop a working methodology for their specific requirements.

The purpose of colour and fashion forecasting is to enable the industry to manufacture products that will be in demand by the consumer at a given period of time in the near future. Meeting this demand ensures the profitability and continued existence of the fashion and textile industry. However, if this demand is not met, then forecasting is failing both the industry and in turn, the whole economy.

Subsequent chapters focus on the decision-making processes or thought patterns that will give depth to the collective body of knowledge of the forecasting process, and show how colour forecasting is meeting consumer demand, if at all. An investigation of suitable methodologies to produce working models of the process will also be introduced.

In this chapter

We have:

- evaluated the importance of colour forecasting for the fashion and textile industry
- assessed the opinions and published evidence of the colour forecasting methodology
- further explored the forecasting process
- discussed the support system of the trade exhibitions
- been introduced to the basic skills of the forecaster
- discovered some useful methods available to the forecaster
- discussed some of the peculiarities of colour.

In the next chapter colour terminology is explained to the reader and the current level of colour knowledge investigated. A colour workshop is incorporated for students wishing to further develop their own colour knowledge.

3 Colour knowledge

Chapter 2 highlighted the importance of hue, intensity and value as three fundamental aspects of colour, particularly relevant to colour forecasting. Colour temperature was also found to be of great significance. These and other important theories, principles and their terminology now need further clarification and understanding to aid the effective compilation of colour stories for forecasting.

Colour knowledge is given little or no attention by writers on colour forecasting. Colour education is quite well introduced in some of the higher education art foundation courses but there are few courses, or even modules within courses – particularly in the area of fashion and textiles – that prepare students for working within the specialist forecasting sector. Colour forecasters can come from a range of educational backgrounds, from fashion, textile or product design to manufacture or even sales and marketing.

Research was undertaken in 2000/2001 into the level of colour knowledge that students bring with them to their courses. It revealed that today's curriculum designers, from primary school onwards, underestimate the importance of understanding basic colour theories and principles. Furthermore, it was found that many students were not fully confident that their colour knowledge was adequate, or even would be by the end of their course. This chapter will enhance your knowledge of colour and boost your confidence in the application of colour, particularly for the compilation of colour stories in forecasting. This vital aspect of forecasting is needed to sell the colour story to potential customers as well as for designers and marketing personnel to explain their stories to colleagues.

In this chapter

We discuss:

- colour history and science and learn about light, vision and additive colour mixing
- the six and twelve-hue colour wheel, exploring subjective colour mixing
- colour terminology and explain its meaning
- colour schemes.

The workshop approach to this chapter will enable you to experiment with colour mixing and colour schemes and appreciate colour and its application in the colour forecasting process.

Colour and light

In 1665 English physicist, mathematician and philosopher Isaac Newton added substantially to the body of scientific knowledge with his discovery of light refraction. He found that natural daylight, or white light, is composed of a spectrum of colours. By projecting light rays onto a solid glass prism, he found that the prism's form separated the combined light energies of different frequencies into a band made up of individual colours. Newton identified seven colours: red, orange, yellow, green, blue, indigo and violet. He showed that this band of colours could be refracted back through a second reversed prism, resulting in a beam of white light. This is illustrated in Figure 3.1.

Newton's discovery superseded the beliefs of the philosophers Pythagoras, Plato and Aristotle, some 2000 years earlier. Pythagoras believed that individual objects emitted their own intrinsic colours making them visible. Plato believed that the eye itself emitted light that reflected colour from the object back to the viewer. Aristotle was the first to realise that light travels in waves and not in particles.

Further investigations led others to conclude that each of the coloured lights had its own wavelength and frequency. Red had the smallest angle of refraction and the longest wavelength, the lowest frequency and the least energy. Violet,

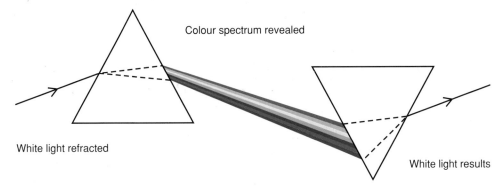

Figure 3.1 A light refraction experiment showing the seven colours of white light: red, orange, yellow, green, blue, indigo and violet, and refracted back through a second prism resulting in a beam of white light.

at the opposite end of the spectrum, with the widest angle of refraction, had the shortest wavelength, highest frequency and most energy.

Light was thus understood to be made up of energy vibrations of differing wavelengths, each perceived by the eye as colour. Colour is therefore an energy vibration with each colour oscillating at a different rate or travelling at a different speed.

In 1887 German physicist Philipp Lenard put forward the theory that electrons emitted from objects absorb light which creates an electric current. In 1900, this was expanded by German physicist Max Planck, who concluded that energy is released and absorbed in small quantities or packets, now known as quanta. This theory formed the basis of Albert Einstein's quantum theory, that light is quanta or photons that move in waves. The distance between successive waves is called the wavelength. Colours are therefore photons of various, but specific, wavelengths. The longer the wavelength, the more spaced out the photons are, resulting in less energy.

The number of times a wave oscillates per second is called the frequency; the longer the wavelength, the lower the frequency. Wavelengths are measured in nanometres (nm). One nanometre is equal to one millionth of a millimetre. The spectrum visible to the human eye is illustrated in Figure 3.2, this is known as the electromagnetic spectrum and shows colour waves in relation to other types of rays.

Amplitude, another measurement of colour, is the height of the wave in relation to its intensity or brightness. The greater the amplitude, the brighter the colour of that wavelength. Brighter colours therefore have a greater amplitude than muted colours.

Colour and vision

In 1802 English physician Thomas Young developed a theory for colour vision that the retina of the human eye receives the light waves and transmits them to the brain through the optic nerves for decoding. The retina comprises around 12 million light-sensitive rods that assist night vision and can discriminate between values of white, grey and black. There are a further six million cones that are sensitive to colour and responsible for our daylight vision. Young's work was continued by German physicist Herman Helmholz in 1867, and in 1871 by Scottish physician James Maxwell. These three sets of work are known as the Tristimulus theory of colour perception and conclude that the cones of the human eye are of three different types, each being capable of receiving one of the three primary colours of light, i.e. red, green and blue. The spectrum visible to the human eye ranges between 760 nm and 380 nm as shown in Figure 3.2.

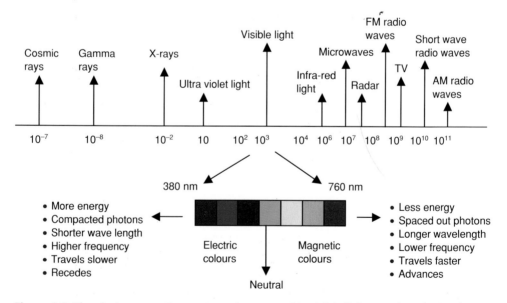

Figure 3.2 The electromagnetic spectrum demonstrating visible light wavelengths in relation to other commonly known wavelengths.

Colour Theories

There are two basic colour theories that we will be discussing: those appertaining to light and those of pigment mixing. While we will focus upon the latter, as do colour forecasters, it is useful to understand the principles of the former. In between these two groups of theories lies a variation that applies to the ink printing used by computer printers. It will also be helpful to discuss this, as computer images are generated using light additive colour mixing on screen but printed out using subtractive colour mixing.

Additive (light) colour theory

Red, green and blue are the primary colours of light and differ slightly from the red, green and blue that are generally associated with the pigment colours we all recognise. This will be discussed later in the chapter on p. 51. The primary light colour red is more orange than the red primary pigment colour. Likewise, the primary light colour green is more yellowy than our normal perception of green; and the light primary colour blue is more of a purple/blue or indigo than the blue we associate with the primary pigment colour.

When more than one of the colours of light are mixed, more light is added and the resulting colour is lighter; this is known as additive mixing. When the three primary colours of light are mixed in equal amounts, the result is white light, as discovered by Newton. Although Newton concluded that all seven colours produce white light, it has since been recognised that only the three primary colours of light are necessary. The primary colours of light are red, green and blue, as shown in Figure 3.3.

Figure 3.3 The primary colours of light: red, green and blue. These differ slightly from the red, green and blue hues that we generally associate with the pigment colours.

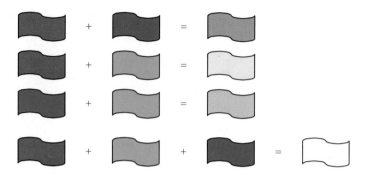

Figure 3.4 The colour mixing combinations of primary light colours to produce the three secondary colours: magenta, yellow and cyan. Adding all three primary colours together results in white light.

The secondary colours of light are known as magenta, yellow and cyan, shown in Figure 3.4. Magenta is made up of equal amounts of primary light colours red and blue. Yellow is a product of equal amounts of red and green. Cyan is the result of equal amounts of blue and green.

Subtractive colour mixing in printing

Computer monitors work on the principle of coloured light, applying additive colour mixing. However, computer printers use a subtractive colour mixing method as for pigments, except the primary colours used by the printer are not red, yellow and blue, but cyan, magenta and yellow – the same as the secondary colours of light, shown in Figure 3.5. Printers do not mix the inks prior to applying them to the paper; instead, the appropriate amount of coloured ink is applied as a separate layer to produce the required colour on paper. As printing inks are transparent and each layer of ink works as a filter, colour reflection is reduced as more layers of ink are applied resulting in a darker colour – which is the principle of subtractive colour mixing.

The secondary colours of the printing inks are red, blue and green – the same as the primary colours of light. Red is the result of mixing magenta and yellow; blue is the result of mixing of magenta and cyan; and green results by mixing cyan and yellow. Superimposing all three primary colours of ink results in black, though it is usual for personal computer printers to use a separate black ink cartridge for a more perfect

Figure 3.5 The three primary colours of ink printers: cyan, magenta and yellow. These are the same as the secondary colours of light but colour mixing is subtractive as with pigment.

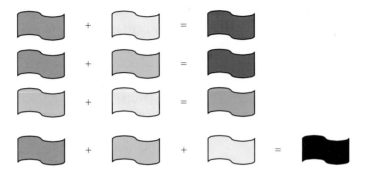

Figure 3.6 The secondary colours of computer printing inks: red, blue and green.

colour. Subtractive colour mixing is shown in Figure 3.6. The white of the printing paper is used for lighter colours and for white; this must be taken into consideration when printing in colour onto coloured paper, as the results will be different to those produced on white paper.

Subtractive mixing (pigment) colour theory

This type of colour mixing will be discussed in more detail than the colour light theory through the introduction of the colour wheel and will carry on through the discussion and experimentation of colour schemes. The mixing of pigments works on the basis of subtractive mixing, like the printing inks but with a different set of primary colours. Much has been published on the application of this theory to paints and pigment dyes. The primary colours of pigments are also different to those of light colour mixing. As with all colour theories, the primary colours cannot be produced by mixing other colours and are only obtainable from a primary source, i.e. plant, mineral or animal.

Colour terminology and the colour wheel

As we have seen, the primary and secondary colours of light and those of pigment mixing are different. From this point onwards we will be discussing and working with only the pigment colours. We will now discuss colour in more detail to further understand the basic terminology useful to the colour forecaster. We will look at how the colour wheel is made up as this is an indispensable tool. You will be encouraged throughout the remainder of this chapter to experiment with colour. A helpful piece of equipment here is a child's paint box containing red, yellow, blue, green, white and black (remember, we are now only working with subtractive colour mixing theory and colours). To create your own colour wheel you will require a circle divided into 12 equal segments to colour in, or you could adopt the style used in Figures 3.7, 3.8 and 3.9, which show the development of the colour wheel using coloured circles. This chapter includes activities designed to expand your colour knowledge they are indicated thus:

Workshop activity

Hue

Hue is the term used to name a colour, i.e. red, yellow, blue. It gives no indication of the exact colour, only the family to which the colour belongs. Other generic names used include pink, brown, turquoise and magenta. Pink belongs to the red family and warm browns belong to the orange family. Turquoise and magenta are generally recognised as two of the six tertiary colours of pigment colour mixing (magenta is a red/violet which looks similar to the magenta referred to previously as a secondary colour of light). However, an exact colour cannot be interpreted from the generic name alone; neither can one determine the composite colour combination of a particular hue without basic colour knowledge. Here lies

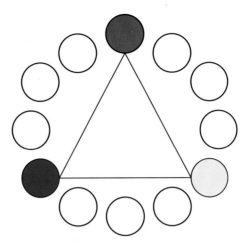

Figure 3.7 The three primary colours evenly spaced on a 12-hue colour wheel. An equilateral triangle can be used to position the colours correctly.

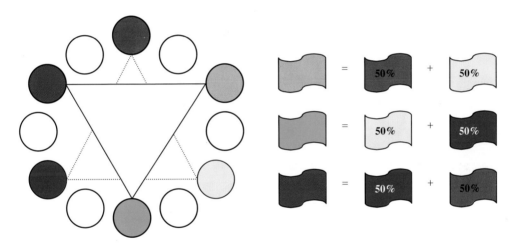

Figure 3.8 Primary and secondary colours on the 12-hue colour wheel and the composition of the secondary colours. The points of the solid upside-down equilateral triangle point to the secondary colours and the points of the broken line equilateral triangle point to the primary colours.

one of the problems that colour communication presents to all those involved in colour and its application. As previously discussed, many colour forecasters claim that hue is less important than the intensity, value and colour temperature aspects of colour even though hue appears to be a prime factor of staple and fashion colours for a season.

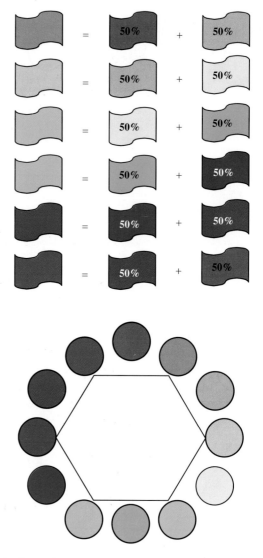

Figure 3.9 The 12-hue colour wheel and the composite colour mixes for the tertiary colours. The points of the hexagram point to the tertiary colours on the wheel.

Workshop activity

Create your own colour wheel, this will be useful for you to keep. Using paper or card, scissors and your paint box, make it BIG, make it **bold**, make it 'yours'. Figure 3.7 is an example, showing the 12 sections you will need. Follow the instructions given in the following workshop activities.

The 12-hue colour wheel

The 12-hue colour wheel is a fundamental tool. It comprises three primary colours, three secondary colours and six tertiary colours. The primary colours are red, yellow and blue, and are evenly spaced around the colour wheel, as shown in Figure 3.7.

Workshop activity

Fill in the primary colours red, yellow and blue on your colour wheel. Refer to Figure 3.7.

The secondary colours are orange, green and violet. These colours contain equal amounts of two primary colours. Orange is made by mixing equal amounts of red and yellow; green is an equal mix of yellow and blue; and violet is made of blue and red. This is shown in Figure 3.8. This figure also shows the secondary and primary colours on the 12-hue colour wheel. These six colours represent the six-hue colour wheel. The six-hue colour wheel contains only the primary and secondary colours, while useful as a colour tool, it is considered that the 12-hue colour wheel is of more benefit to the user as the six tertiary colours are a representation of the colours between those of the six-hue colour wheel. The six-hue colour wheel will be referred to again later in the chapter. The 12-hue colour wheel is generally con-sidered to be a more useful tool as the tertiary colours are included.

Workshop activity

Experiment mixing secondary colours until you are happy with the result. Some childrens' paint palettes include a green, which you can use if you wish; but try mixing yellow and blue to produce your own greens anyway! Refer to Figure 3.8.

The next six colours complete the 12-hue colour wheel and are the tertiary colours: red/orange, orange/yellow, yellow/green, green/blue, blue/violet and violet/red. Each tertiary colour is made up of one primary colour and one adjacent secondary colour on the colour wheel. As each secondary colour is made up of a 50/50 mix of two primary colours, a tertiary colour is made up of a total of 75% of one primary colour and 25% of another. This is true when the mid-way colour is the representative (as on the 12-hue colour wheel); however, many combinations are possible that lie between each of these 12 colours. Figure 3.9 shows the simplified compositions of the tertiary colours and the full 12-hue colour wheel, where the points of the hexagram indicate the tertiary colours.

Workshop activity

Have fun experimenting with the tertiary colours. Add them to your colour wheel. Refer to Figure 3.9.

In reality, a tertiary colour can be made up of any combination of primary colours plus a secondary colour. There are generic names that are generally used for all of the tertiary colours, with the exception of red/orange, which is referred to as scarlet or salmon or other names according to fashion trends or personal perception. Commonly used generic names for the tertiary colours are scarlet, gold, lime, turquoise, indigo and magenta (see Figure 3.10). More divisions in each of the 12 hues are achieved by altering the composition of the primary

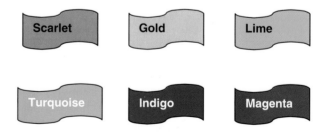

Figure 3.10 The six tertiary colours and examples of some of the generic names often given to these hues.

and secondary colours (shown in Figure 3.10). For example, 70% blue and 30% green will result in a more blue turquoise than the turquoise hue on the colour wheel.

Workshop activity

Play around with variations of tertiary colours that could be placed between the colours of the 12-hue colour wheel. This will help to boost your confidence in colour mixing and improve your appreciation of colour composition. The main thing is to enjoy this activity.

The 12-hue colour wheel is a simple workable tool. Colour names are often used by forecasters to set the mood for a given colour story. These names may be reused for a different season, applied to a slightly different hue, or the same hue may be given an updated generic name to suggest freshness to a range of colours.

Workshop activity

Think up names for the range of colours you produced in the previous workshop activity. Put yourself in the colour forecaster's shoes and try selecting appropriate names for your colours – take time on this and be creative. Add more colours to your collection if you wish.

Intensity

Intensity is the strength of a colour. This may also be referred to as a colour's saturation or brightness. A pure hue can be fully saturated or less saturated without altering the hue itself, only its strength. Another important factor is the reflection of light from different fibres, yarns and fabrics. Fibres with high lustre such as silk – and the many man-made fibres that imitate the characteristics of silk – give the impression of full saturation; whereas opaque fibres, such as wool, generally give colours with less saturation. Advancements in the dyeing

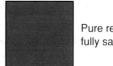

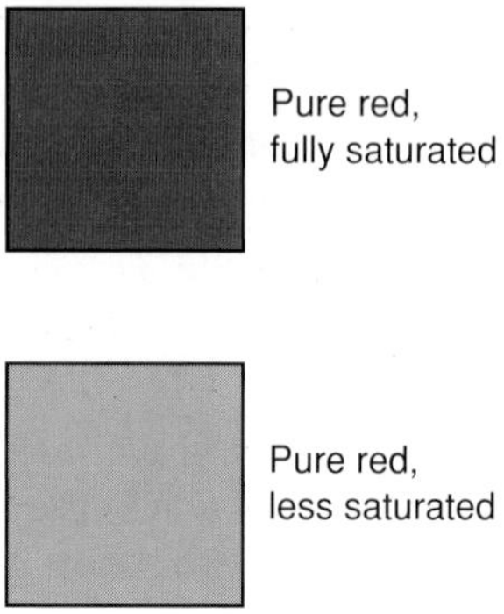

Pure red,
fully saturated

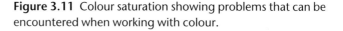

Pure red,
less saturated

Figure 3.11 Colour saturation showing problems that can be encountered when working with colour.

and finishing industry have more or less overcome this problem and stronger, brighter colours can now be achieved on opaque fibres such as wool. Without this ability, some fibres would become unpopular during periods of certain colour trends. Saturation of the colour red is demonstrated in Figure 3.11, where the option on the computer was used to select a less saturated hue. However, the less saturated red may be perceived as a red/orange. Also remember that computer printer inks are transparent and selecting an option for less saturation allows more of the paper colour to show through. This highlights the problems encountered by those working in the field of colour, particularly when working with computer generated and printed material.

Workshop activity

Experiment using varying amounts of water to dilute your paints to adjust the saturation or intensity of the colours. Refer to Figure 3.11.

Value

The value of a colour is its clarity or purity. Pure colours have no added white, black, or grey and are often termed as brights; whereas colours with an added amount of white are known as tints. Colours with an added amount of black are known as shades and those with an added amount of grey are known as tones and are often referred to as muted. Many variations of a hue can be achieved by altering the value so this is an important aspect for the colour forecaster to consider.

The value of each primary, secondary and tertiary colour can be altered, according to the percentage of tonal value added. Values alone can be used as colours with no added hue and these are known as achromatics. Their generic names are white, grey and black. Grey may be of any combination of white and black and fashion names are often given, such as slate and silver. Figure 3.12 illustrates the values: tints, tones and shades.

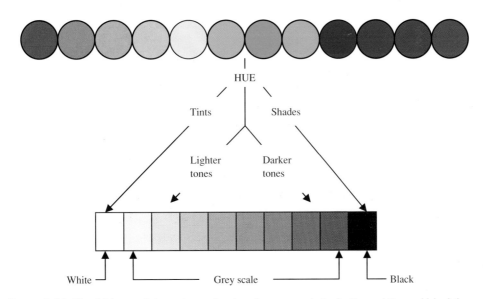

Figure 3.12 The 12 hues of the colour wheel and a grey scale including white and black for the mixing of tones, tints and shades respectively.

Workshop activity

Play with grey! Mix light greys, medium greys, dark greys. Add more water to change the saturation. Be creative, give your colour samples names. Refer to the grey scale in Figure 3.12.

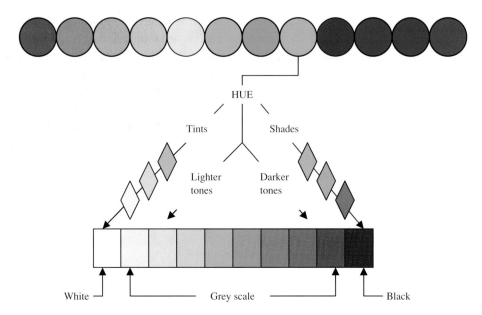

Figure 3.13 Turquoise from the 12-hue colour wheel applied to white, black and grey to demonstrate some of the different tints, shades and tones achievable when mixing a hue with different values.

Tones may be light, moderate or dark, depending on the amount of black and white used, e.g. more white produces lighter tones. Equal amounts of black and white produce more moderate tones. Figure 3.13 shows the colour blue/green (turquoise) superimposed onto the tints, tones and shades.

Workshop activity

Mix different values of grey, white and black to the 12 hues of the colour wheel. This will help you to appreciate the colour composition of tints, tones and shades. Refer to Figure 3.13. Notice how the colours change, revealing the richness of shades, the lightness of tints and the misty qualities of the tones. Try naming some of your new colour combinations.

There are few generic names for tints, tones and shades of hues. Some used include navy (blue shade), burgundy (red shade), pink (red tint), peach (orange tint), and khaki (yellow tone). Tints are often referred to as pastels and they create lighter weight colours than tones and shades. Tones are also called muted colours: light tones appear misty; dark tones also appear misty but heavier than light ones. Shades appear heavier than the other values and are sometimes referred to as darks, or dark colours. These are often rich in appearance. No specific tool exists for identifying these variations of value commonly used by the forecasters. However, a system was devised by Eric Danger in 1987 showing variations of composition of hue and value. This could help the colour worker identify the fine line between what are generally termed light, medium and dark values as well as to help to communicate intensity and colour clarity. Bright or pure hues tend to be clear while tonal colours are muted.

Colour temperature

Red, orange and yellow hues are generally described as warm, and green, blue and violet are cool hues. Red is generally considered to be warmer than yellow and blue is considered the coolest of the pure hues. Figure 3.14 shows the warm and cool hues of the 12-hue colour wheel. In particular yellow and violet are often thought of as temperate colours, that is neither predominantly warm nor cool. This is also said of yellow/green and violet/red, depending upon the undertone of the individual colour. Undertones are discussed next.

Workshop activity

Examine your range of colours: are all the reds warm looking? Are all your blues cool? Take a good look. You may find some of those that should appear warm are not as warm looking as others, likewise with the cool colours. Refer to the next section and to Figures 3.15 to 3.19 for a better understanding of the complexities of colour temperature.

Undertones

Each hue has an undertone, which is its underlying primary colour. It is the undertone of a hue that determines its temperature. A blue undertone gives a hue a cool bias and a red

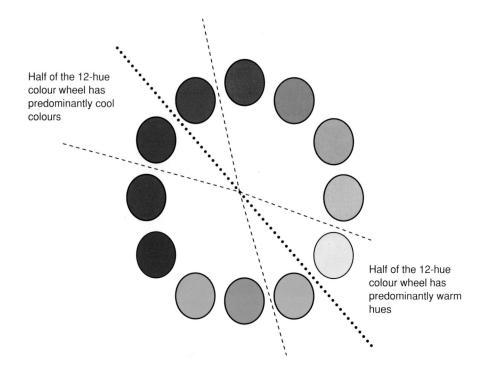

Half of the 12-hue
colour wheel has
predominantly cool
colours

Half of the 12-hue
colour wheel has
predominantly warm
hues

Figure 3.14 The warm and cool colours on the 12-hue colour wheel, though the colours on either side of the black dotted line – yellow, yellow/green, violet and violet/red – are commonly thought of as more temperate hues. That is to say, neither predominantly warm nor cool.

one gives it a warm bias. Each hue can have either a warm or a cool undertone, regardless of the actual hue. Therefore blue, although generally a cool colour, can have a warm bias if the undertone is red. This is also true of the warm hue red, which with a blue undertone becomes cool. Thus each primary hue can have a warm and a cool variation.

If two primary colours with a warm bias are combined, a warm biased secondary colour will result (see Figure 3.15). Similarly, if two primary colours with a cool bias are mixed, a secondary colour with a cool bias will result (see Figure 3.16). However, mixing colours with a different colour temperature bias will result in a more temperate secondary colour. Figures 3.17, 3.18 and 3.19 show the colour temperature bias of secondary colours orange, green and violet respectively, produced by mixing two primaries – one with a warm bias and one with a cool bias. However, the hues will still be considered warm or cool in accordance with Figure 3.14.

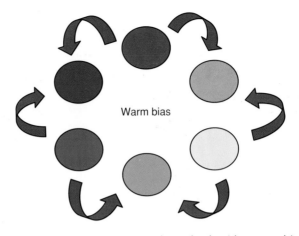

Figure 3.15 Mixing two primary colours, both with a warm bias or undertone will always result in a warm biased secondary hue.

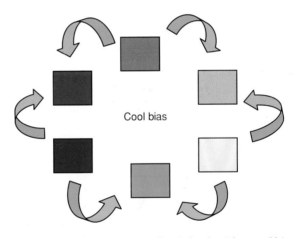

Figure 3.16 Mixing two primary colours, both with a cool bias or undertone will always result in a cool biased secondary hue.

Figures 3.15 to 3.19 show secondary hues with a cool, warm or temperate colour temperature bias. In principle, the combination of two warm primaries will result in a warm secondary hue. Likewise, two cool primaries mixed together theoretically create a cool secondary hue; and a cool and a warm primary hue mixed will result in a more temperate secondary hue. In reality however, the colour temperature of a hue depends on the percentage of warm and cool hue biases of the undertones.

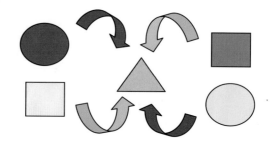

Figure 3.17 Mixing a warm red and a cool yellow will result in a temperate orange. The same results from mixing a cool red and a warm yellow. Hues shown in circles denote warm hues, cool hues are shown in squares and the temperate results are shown as triangular.

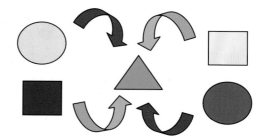

Figure 3.18 Mixing a warm yellow and a cool blue will result in a temperate green. The same results from mixing a cool yellow and a warm blue.

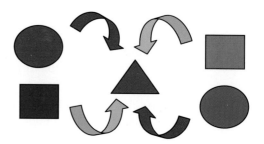

Figure 3.19 Mixing a warm red and a cool blue will result in a temperate violet. The same results from mixing a cool red and a warm blue.

Neutrals

Neutrals, or neutral colours, are sometimes referred to as earth tones. Each neutral is a combination of all three primary colours of any percentage mix. As with any other colour, the dominant undertone will determine the colour temperature. Neutrals are often muddy in appearance as they are produced by mixing colours that are opposite on the colour wheel – known as complementary colours – which effectively cancels each other out when mixed (colour complementaries are discussed later on p. 70). Theoretically, this cancellation produces non-colour, i.e. black. In reality, because colours are never 100% pure but contain some impurities, the result is not black but a dirty nondescript colour (just like the water you wash your paint brush in when mixing or using many different colours). For instance, a neutral may be produced by mixing complementary colours orange and blue. Orange is made up of the two primary colours red and yellow, blue is the third primary colour. The result of mixing these two colours would be a neutral of some kind but in fact the resulting colour will depend upon the amounts of each primary colour in the mix. Figure 3.20 shows the difference in hue between a neutral colour made by mixing all three primary colours and a brown that some may confuse as a neutral that is in actual fact a shade of orange, i.e. red + yellow + black.

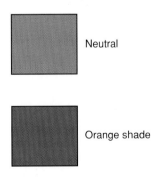

Neutral

Orange shade

Figure 3.20 The difference between a neutral colour and a brown (orange shade).

Workshop activity

Experiment mixing neutrals, first using all three primary colours and then with combinations of yellow and purple; red and green; blue and orange.

As with pure hues, achromatic values (i.e. black, white and grey; see p. 67 for explanation) can also be added to a neutral, producing more variations of colour. However, as neutrals are by nature muddy in appearance, and greys and white are somewhat misty, the addition of these values may not produce very appealing colours, particularly for fashion apparel.

Workshop activity

Experiment further with neutrals, adding white, black and greys to your neutral combinations. Can you give these new colours exciting names? Can you feel the colour temperature of these colours? Can you appreciate their colour composition?
Well done!
You should now understand the important principles of colour mixing and colour composition. If you have completed the workshop activities so far, you are also becoming familiar with the colour forecasting process and have enhanced your understanding.

Colour schemes

There are some rules designers use to create colour combinations that are very useful for the student to understand. The role of the colour forecaster is to compile colour stories that are harmonious, incorporating colours that work well together as trend prediction packages. Designers then use trend predictions along with other sources of inspiration to create product ranges that complement each other. This helps consumers to mix and match more confidently and potentially generates more sales.

Monochromatics

Monochromatic colour schemes comprise two or more colours that are variations of one hue. These colour combinations are considered to be harmonious due to the colour relationship. An example of a monochromatic colour scheme is shown in Figure 3.21. Achromatics are colour combinations based on black, white or grey. An example of an achromatic colour scheme is shown in Figure 3.22. Strong contrasts can be

Figure 3.21 A monochromatic colour scheme based on blue/green (turquoise).

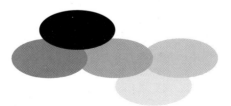

Figure 3.22 An achromatic colour scheme using four tonal greys and black.

achieved using colour combinations of shades and tints and more subtle combinations can be created with different saturations of hue.

Analogous colour schemes

Analogous colour schemes are harmonious combinations, linked by a common colour. These colours are either next to each other on the colour wheel, or very close. Using the 12-hue colour wheel, the analogous colours of red are considered to be red/orange and red/violet as these are directly next to red. When using the six-hue colour wheel, the colours directly next to red are orange and violet, which are therefore considered to be analogous hues of red. In addition to these four colours, orange/yellow and violet/blue are also analogous colours of red as they both contain a degree of red. The importance of analogous colour combinations is the relationship to each other through one colour, so they do not necessarily appear directly next to each other on the colour wheel.

Analogous colour schemes may comprise two colours (dyads), three (triads), four (tetrads) or more, for example pentads (5) and hexads (6). Colours may be directly next to each other on the colour wheel or more widely spread, as long as there is a colour relationship common to all the colours of the combination. Figure 3.23 shows four examples of analogous dyads. Greater contrasts can be achieved between two colours of different colour temperature. Colours next to each other on the six-hue colour wheel have a greater contrast than those on the 12-hue colour wheel. Figure 3.24 shows an example of an analogous dyad using two colours of different colour temperature and also a tetrad again demonstrating the effect of using differences of colour temperature.

Workshop activity

Using your collection of colour samples, play around with analogous dyad combinations. Start with bright colours, then introduce tints, tones and shades. Refer to Figures 3.23 and 3.24. Ensure the colour combinations have a colour relationship, then experiment with triad analogous colour combinations, with tetrads and more colours if you wish.

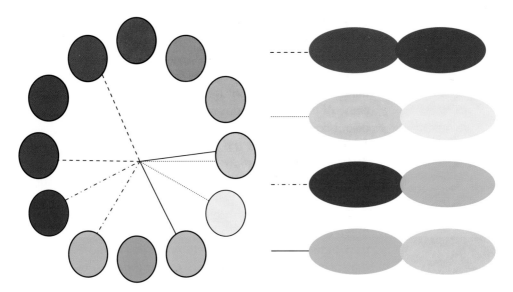

Figure 3.23 Four dyad analogous colour schemes. The first, have violet in common. The second pair of colours have yellow in common and are next to each other on the 12-hue colour wheel. Similarly the third pair appear together on the colour wheel and have blue in common. The final pair both contain yellow.

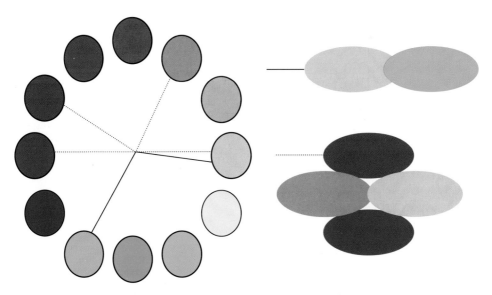

Figure 3.24 A dyad analogous combination using two colours of different colour temperature for greater effect, yellow/orange (gold) and blue/green (turquoise), both containing yellow. The second combination is a tetrad with a red relationship. The cooler blue/violet adds interest to the warmer hues of the combination.

Complementary colour schemes

Complementary colours are opposites on the colour wheel. Complementary colour schemes are also considered to be harmonious, though not through colour relationship but because of their harmonious contrast. This is particularly true of colour complementaries on the six-hue colour wheel. On the 12-hue colour wheel the additional set of complementaries do have a colour relationship, though in very small measure. The complementary pairs red/orange and blue/green both have a small amount of yellow; yellow/orange and blue/violet share a common link through the colour red; and yellow/green and red/violet both have some blue content. The contrast between these complementaries is therefore less than that of complementary colours red and green, orange and blue, and yellow and violet where there is no colour relationship. All of these dyad complementaries are considered to be harmonious. Figure 3.25 shows four sets of complementary pairs. Complementary pairs can be enhanced by changing the tonal value of one or both of the colours.

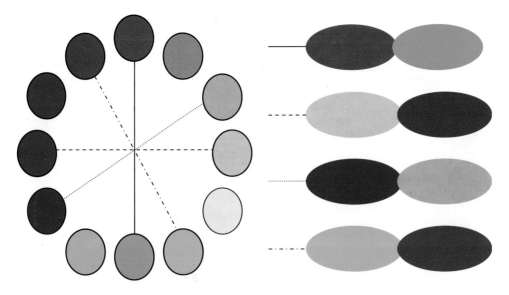

Figure 3.25 Four complementary pairs. The first (red and green) and the third (blue and orange), have no colour relationship, therefore they are purely harmonious contrasts. The second colour combination (yellow/orange and blue/violet), have red as a common colour, so the colours are still considered to be complementary pairs and not analogous, as they are opposite on the colour wheel. The final pair (yellow/green and red/violet), have blue as the common colour relationship.

It is possible to create a triad using two complementary colours plus a different value of one of the complementary pair as the third colour. Other combinations can be created using this principle for tetrads, pentads and hexads. Some examples are shown in Figures 3.26 and 3.27.

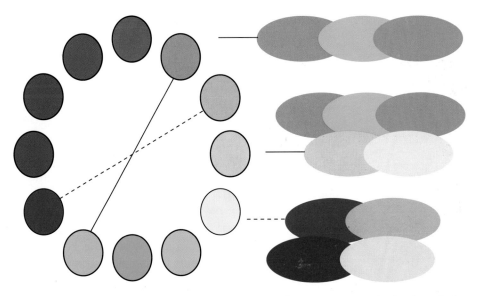

Figure 3.26 Three colour combinations based on complementary pairs. The first is a triad using red/orange and blue/green. A shade of blue/green has been added in the first instance. The second combination is an extension of the first adding two varying orange tints to create a pentad combination. The final colour range is a tetrad using the complementary pair blue and orange. The additional two colours are a blue shade and an orange tint.

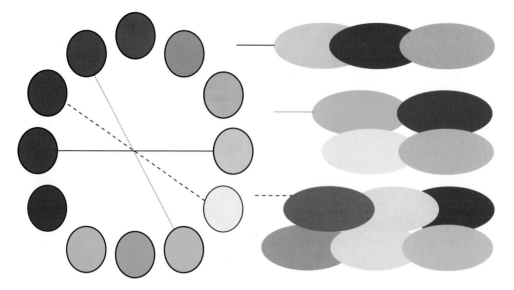

Figure 3.27 Three colour ranges, the first, a triad using orange/yellow and blue/violet. A slight blue/violet tint has been added to the complementary pair. The second group of colours comprises the complementaries yellow/green and red/violet. Two red/violet tints have been added, one much lighter than the other, to make a tetrad combination. The final combination is a hexad using yellow and violet. There is no colour relationship common to this complementary pair. Yellow, two different yellow shades and two violet tints, the lighter slightly tonal have been added to make this colour combination.

Split complementaries

Another type of triad using complementary principles is known as a split complementary colour scheme. Instead of using a hue and its complementary colour, this combination uses the two hues either side of the complementary colour. Again, changing the value of one or more of the three hues will add more possibilities. Examples of split complementary colour combinations are shown in Figures 3.28 and 3.29. On the six-hue colour wheel the combinations are either the primary colours (red, yellow and blue) or the secondary colours (orange, green and violet). Combinations using the 12-hue colour wheel are less contrasting (for example, red, yellow/green and blue/green; or yellow/orange, blue and violet), as there is a slight colour relationship between at least two of the colours within the colour combination.

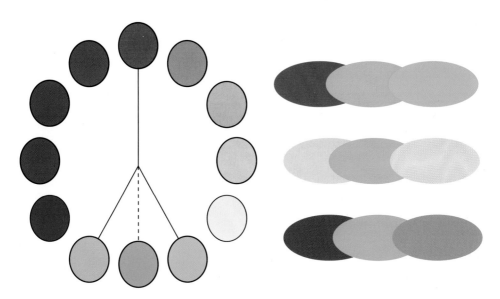

Figure 3.28 Variations of a split complementary using red, blue/green and yellow/green, as shown on the colour wheel. Three combinations of three colours are shown: first in the original state; secondly, the values of red and yellow/green have been changed to tints of the same; and the third group of colours shows a slight blue/green shade, and red and yellow/green shades.

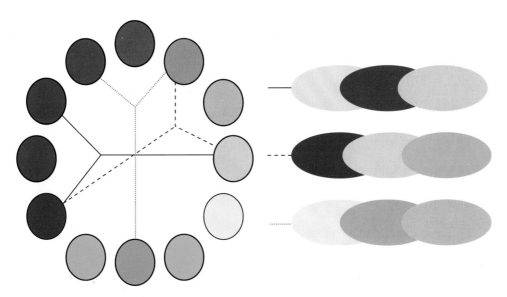

Figure 3.29 Three different split complementary colour combinations. The first group of three colours are orange/yellow and split complementaries, blue and violet. The blue and orange/yellow have been tinted. The second combination shows blue and its split complementary colours, red/orange and orange/yellow. The two complementaries have been altered: the red/orange is a tint and the orange/yellow is slightly tonal. The third colour combination uses the split complementaries of green, red/orange and red/violet. The green and red/violet have been altered to tints and the red/orange is a light tone.

Workshop activity

Experiment with split complementaries. Refer to Figures 3.28 and 3.29.

Double split complementaries

Apart from using additional values of one or more of the complementary hues to make a tetrad colour combination, there are two specific types of combination using complementaries. The first is known as a double split complementary, where one of the hues either side of the first hue is used and one of the colours on one side of the complementary hue is used. This is usually identified by an oblong within the hub of the colour wheel. This is shown in Figure 3.30.

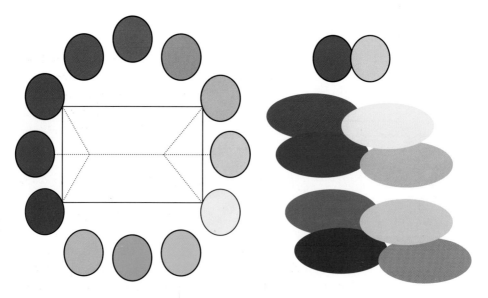

Figure 3.30 A double split complementary combination using an oblong in the hub of the colour wheel. The first pair of colours are the selected complementary pair. The first tetrad shows the two sets of split complementary colours: violet, orange, yellow and blue in their original state. The second tetrad shows variations of the first tetrad. The violet has been tinted and the rest are shades.

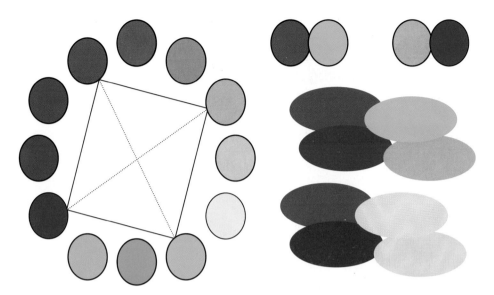

Figure 3.31 Two hues, red/violet and blue and their complementary colours yellow/green and orange, respectively, and shown by the use of a square in the hub of the colour wheel. The first tetrad colour combination shows the four colours in their original state. The second tetrad demonstrates one of the possibilities achievable by changing the values. Red/violet orange and yellow/green have been changed to tints, and the blue to a slight shade.

The second tetrad colour combination method using two pairs of complementaries utilises a square in the hub of the colour wheel to select colours of equal distance; for this reason it is not possible on the six-hue wheel. This method of colour selection is shown in Figure 3.31 where the colour relationship in the colour combination is evident. There is blue, green/yellow, red/violet and orange; three of the colours contain blue, two contain red and two contain yellow. This colour combination thus contains a measure of all the primary colours.

There is also a variation of the double split where a trapezoid is placed into the hub of the colour wheel to select the colours. First we select a colour, then determine this hue's two split complementaries. This is shown in Figure 3.32, where green has been selected, the complementary is red and the split complementary colours are red/violet and red/orange; these are now the first two colours of the combination.

We now use one of the split complementaries of each of these hues – in this case red, red/violet and red/orange. The complementary of red/violet is green/yellow and the

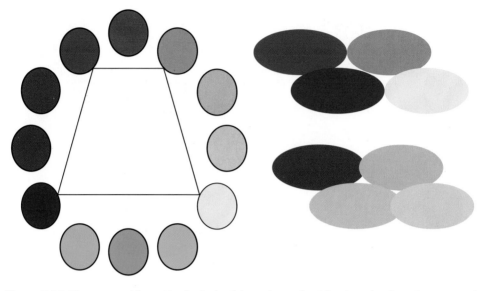

Figure 3.32 The trapezoid used in the hub of the colour wheel for the selection of two sets of complementary pairs. The first tetrad shows the four colours in their original state. The second group shows changes to the values of three of the hues. Red/orange has been changed to a tint; blue and yellow to light tones; the red/violet remains unchanged.

split complementary colours are green and yellow. To form the trapezoid shape we need to select the yellow. Likewise, the complementary colour of red/orange is blue/green, split complementaries of blue/green are blue and green, and to complete the trapezoid we select blue.

This process demonstrates the principle behind colour combination, and rather than try to memorise the process, simply use the trapezoid shape. The method does not incorporate any complementary pairs at all in the colour combination, it just uses them as a basis for the selection. There is some degree of colour relationship between the four resulting colours.

Workshop activity

Experiment with tetrad colour combinations using the square, the oblong and the trapezoid. Refer to Figures 3.30 to 3.32.

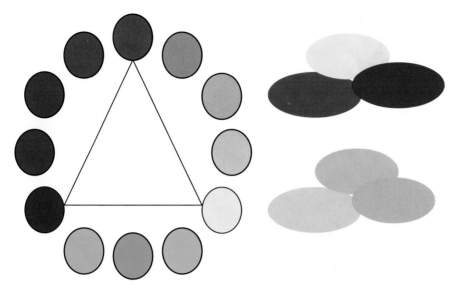

Figure 3.33 An equilateral triangle in the hub of the colour wheel for colour selection. The first triad colour combination shows the three primary colours in their original state. The second triad shows the colours with changed values. The red has been changed to a tint and the blue and yellow to tones.

There is one more harmonious triad to understand that uses an equilateral triangle in the hub of the colour wheel to select three colours of equal distance. On the six-hue colour wheel there are two combinations: red, yellow and blue – the primary colours; and orange, green and violet – the secondary colours. There are an additional two combinations when using the 12-hue colour wheel: red/violet, blue/green and orange/yellow; and red/orange, yellow/green and blue/violet. These combinations are shown in Figure 3.33; again the values can be changed by adding black, white or grey to one or more of the colours of the combination.

Discordant colour schemes

Most colour schemes are considered to be harmonious but there are some that are considered to be discordant – this does not necessarily mean undesirable. There is also a recognised rule of harmony or discord when broken from a natural order of colour. When using the complementary pair yellow and violet, the yellow is naturally lighter. If white is added to

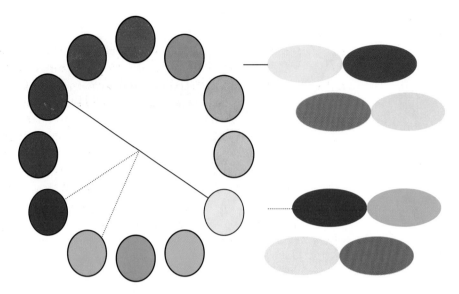

Figure 3.34 Examples of discordant colour combinations. The first pair of the first group of four colours are shown in their natural state and order. The second pair of this group have been changed to yellow shade and violet tint, thus reversing the natural order of the colours to create a discordant pair. Similarly, the second group of four colours shows the natural order of the colours blue and blue/green. Changing these hues to light tonal blue and a blue/green shade alters the natural colour order.

the violet and black to the yellow, this changes the natural order and is considered to be discordant. Examples are shown in Figure 3.34.

Another example of discord is where two colours do not share the same value, for example pink and brown. Pink is red and white; brown is orange and black. Again the results may not necessarily be undesirable.

Workshop activity

Experiment with discordant colour combinations. Refer to Figure 3.34. Decide for yourself each combination's desirability.

Clash

A clash combination is another example of discord. This combination is similar to a split complementary colour scheme but using only one of the split complementary colours. For example, red and green/yellow. On the 12-hue colour wheel the clash colour is related to the complementary colour and all three primary colours are present in the combination. The clash contrast is greater using the six-hue colour wheel where these combinations will be either the three primary colours – red, yellow and blue where the contrast is greatest, or the three secondary colours – orange, green and violet. Finally, achromatic hues and neutrals may be added to any of the above combinations adding one or more colours to the scheme.

Workshop activity

Look at wallpaper samples, fabrics, packaging, etc. and try to work out the colour combinations used. Decide whether you feel they work or not and why. Try not to let personal preferences influence your judgement. This is an important exercise to help you to develop the colour awareness skills essential for colour forecasting.

Metamerism

As a final but important comment, let us return to the section where we discussed light and how it is made up of various colours. The wavelength components of light will vary depending on the time of day, weather and the location in the world; in other words, natural light varies. Artificial light also varies enormously, both from natural light and from other artificial lights. These variations can have a dramatic effect on the perceived colour of a product and this is known as metamerism. Our parents and grandparents were aware of this effect and would never consider buying a garment without having taken it out of the store to view in natural daylight. Modern security systems make this impossible today. Dyestuff manufacturers and the textile industry in general have spent considerable time and money tackling this issue but metamerism is important for the designer and colour forecaster to be aware of.

Workshop activity

Select three or more strongly coloured garments from your wardrobe. View each of these under artificial light in the home, again outside in the natural light and finally under the artificial lighting in at least one large store. Note carefully the differences you observe in the colour of each garment. You could also compare a colour in natural daylight on a bright sunny day and on a grey cloudy day. Maybe you have bought a garment abroad and not liked the colour so much when you got it back home. This all demonstrates the importance of the effect of light on colour – in other words, of metamerism.

Summary

More information on colour and its application is needed by students on fashion and textile related courses, as well as in other design disciplines. In this chapter we have addressed this need, through both discussion and practical workshop activities. This will have provided a better understanding of the colour terminology used by the colour forecaster and have deepened the level of knowledge of the future professionals of this field.

Colour is a major component of fashion and there is no doubt that the fashion and textile industry needs advance indications of the colours that consumers will desire. The more involved an individual becomes in working with colour, the greater is their awareness of colour: this awareness is vital to the forecaster. The practical exercises within this chapter will have also helped sharpen that awareness.

This chapter has introduced the basic colour knowledge essential to those embarking on a career involving colour forecasting, whether in the specialist sector or as a designer or buyer. Forecasters do not consciously use colour schemes for the development of colour stories but their natural flair for colour is likely to be subconsciously based upon the principles of colour harmony. Understanding these principles will certainly help the forecaster, and particularly students developing their own talent for mood board and colour story development.

In this chapter

We have:

- been introduced to light and colour vision to understand the principles of light theory
- developed an understanding of colour mixing, both additive and subtractive
- achieved a deeper understanding of colour terminology used by the colour forecaster
- discussed and developed the 12-hue colour wheel
- achieved an understanding of colour composition and colour schemes essential for the compilation of colour stories.

In the next chapter we will look at the process of colour forecasting holistically to understand fully what the forecasters do and how they do it. The remaining chapters are more specific to the process of colour forecasting and the practical aspects of designing good mood boards and colour stories.

4 The colour forecasting process

Now that we have a clearer understanding of the colour terminology used by the colour forecasters and a richer knowledge of colour itself, we can focus upon the process of colour forecasting. In this chapter we look at the process as a whole, and in Chapters 5 and 6 we will break this down to look deeper into the thought and decision-making in compiling colour stories.

It is difficult to find any book which clearly defines the stages of colour forecasting but a model of any process enables us to understand it more clearly. We will look at a model of the general practice currently employed throughout the fashion and textile industry and compare this with a proposed improved model. We do this using elements of a modelling tool known as soft systems methodology (SSM), widely employed in investigating human behaviour.

Soft systems thinking was a useful tool to use in investigating the colour forecasting industry and to develop two models. The first of these models expresses the methodology as currently used and the second expresses what we consider to be an improved approach. These models were used to survey the UK fashion and textile industry in order to test their validity. Once analysed and interpreted, the survey results suggested that the models were easy to understand and that the response rate was good. The models were refined using feedback from the survey and consumer opinion was also tested, stressing the need to improve the current colour forecasting process.

We have seen from the background presented in Chapter 1, that colour forecasting provides a tool to help the fashion and textile industry make the correct colour choices for their products. However, it is evident that a potentially valuable source of information has not yet been fully exploited, that of market research to investigate and understand consumer colour preference, desire or need.

In this chapter

We shall increase our knowledge of the colour forecasting process currently used in the fashion and textile industry, discuss the weaknesses of this system and make suggestions for improvement. This will be achieved through:

- a deeper understanding of the colour forecasting process using a model
- discussion of how effective the process is and how it could be improved
- presenting a revised model of a more effective system to benefit both the industry and the consumer.

The process explained

Colour forecasting provides:

- an evaluation and analysis of the possible colour preferences of consumers for a season approximately two years ahead of the retail season, giving ample time to fit into the production schedules of the industry
- a service enabling the presentation and sale of this information to the fashion and textile industry.

Colour forecasting is carried out worldwide by individuals working for specialist forecasting companies who will sell a limited colour story on a seasonal basis to the fashion and textile industry. The colour forecasting process and service thus promotes a selection of colours for a predetermined time period in the near future for all sectors of the fashion and textile industry. The forecasts predict colours through a complex mixture of intuition and analysis. The information is used by those responsible for the colour decisions of their company's products.

Who uses the colour forecasting process?

Colour forecasters work in many different parts of the industry. This is illustrated in Figure 4.1 which shows forecasters who work with the colour forecasting process from the

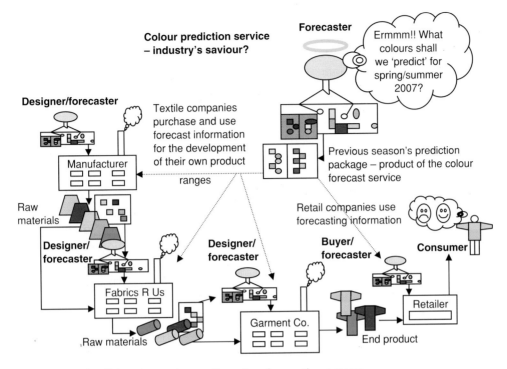

Figure 4.1 Identifying those who use the colour forecasting process.

initial concept (the original colour forecasters) through to the consumer of the end product.

At the early stages of the process there are those who provide the service to the industry, known as the colour forecasting companies. Thereafter the information users become less and less involved, starting with the fibre, yarn and fabric producers, followed by the garment manufacturers, and finally the retailers. Often, designers and product buyers take on the role of forecasting as they are responsible for their company's colour choices. Large companies generally have a team of people working together to compile their colour stories; smaller companies may have only one person responsible for this – usually the designer.

The first level of information users is that of the fibre and yarn manufacturers who supply the fabric manufacturers and knitwear companies. The fabric manufacturers supply the garment making industry, and both the knitwear companies and the garment manufacturers supply the retailers. The fibre and yarn manufacturers use colour forecasting information to help them to compile their own prediction packages in the form of shade cards with sales data usually influencing their choice of colour. The major companies' colour teams all regularly attend national and international colour meetings.

Fabric and knitwear manufacturers use both colour forecasting information and fibre and yarn company shade cards to direct their colour choices, and this information is well disseminated via trade exhibitions. Garment manufacturers also utilise both forecasting information and shade cards; retailers will make use of forecasting information along with information gathered from trade fairs. Retailers may also use sales data, particularly large companies using EPOS (electronic point of sale) systems. No evidence has been found of collecting colour data, nor any indication of who could take on its analysis. This is a major source of information not presently exploited.

The consumer may be influenced by colour trends promoted through magazines and television but does not have access to the trade forecasting information. It is consumers, however, who prove the effectiveness of colour forecasting predictions by what they buy. The consumer is observed by the colour forecasters, thereby involving them in the process albeit without them realising it.

How colour forecasting is perceived

There are two basic views of the colour forecasting process: the positive and the negative. Those endorsing the positive view perceive the process as a tool used by a specialist service sector to provide accurate trend prediction information to the fashion and textile industry, enabling the user to anticipate accurately consumer colour preferences for a predetermined season in the near future. This allows the industry to manufacture desirably coloured products for the benefit of both the company and the consumer.

Those taking the more negative view see colour forecasting as a process used by a service sector to exploit the fashion and textile industry for financial benefit, and to dupe the general public by its attempts to direct consumer preferences with clever marketing. This negative interpretation is perhaps extreme but may be happening by default, despite the best intentions of the forecasters. A high volume of sales on the high street will confirm the forecasters' ability for getting it right, instilling confidence in the service. Low sales however, will weaken the credibility of the forecast predictions, generating a lack of confidence in both the service and the process.

In reality, it is probably a combination of the two perspectives that prevails. The tangible, objective tools instill confidence, while the less understood, subjective ones create suspicion. Good marketing engenders optimism but a low volume of sales on the high street leads to pessimism. If the 'softer' elements of the process were better understood and the forecasting process as a whole demonstrated a higher success rate, forecasters would be perceived as beneficial to the industry. Colour forecasting may thus be seen as a process that has potential to assist the fashion and textile industry to thrive but is as yet little understood, so remains underdeveloped and its value consequently underestimated.

Two further points for consideration are those of consumer lifestyles and mass customisation and how they add to the perception of trend forecasting. Consumer lifestyles are much investigated and their significance now recognised as a key influencer of marketing. Companies base their product range on customer profiles created from lifestyle information. But what of colour preferences? Consumers can only choose to buy or not buy the products on offer at that moment in time, expressing their acceptance of the products offered. If lifestyles are so important to marketing, why is colour preference data not felt to be beneficial? Why is the industry still so reliant upon the forecasters' anticipations of colour acceptance? Mass customisation is the large-scale manufacturing of individual consumer products. Whether or not this approach is viable is not the issue but it does suggest that the industry may not be completely satisfied that the present forecasting service is as accurate in its predictions as it could be. Accuracy is crucial to the survival of the industry.

The responsibility for colour direction

The onus for the direction of colour initially rested with the primary market sector; i.e. the fibre, yarn and fabric manufacturers. They produce the colours of the raw materials that the rest of the fashion and textile industry use. Yet the retailers clearly have more access to information on consumer buying behaviour and selection preferences through sales data, observation and feedback communicated from the shop floor. Four areas of the industry are illustrated in Figure 4.2, referred

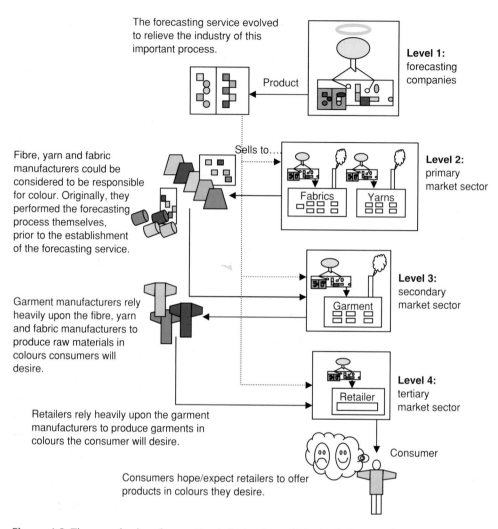

The forecasting service evolved to relieve the industry of this important process.

Product

Level 1: forecasting companies

Sells to...

Level 2: primary market sector

Fibre, yarn and fabric manufacturers could be considered to be responsible for colour. Originally, they performed the forecasting process themselves, prior to the establishment of the forecasting service.

Fabrics

Yarns

Level 3: secondary market sector

Garment manufacturers rely heavily upon the fibre, yarn and fabric manufacturers to produce raw materials in colours consumers will desire.

Garment

Level 4: tertiary market sector

Retailer

Retailers rely heavily upon the garment manufacturers to produce garments in colours the consumer will desire.

Consumer

Consumers hope/expect retailers to offer products in colours they desire.

Figure 4.2 The use of colour forecasting information within the fashion and textile industry.

to as Levels 1 to 4: the forecasting sector; the fibre, fabric and yarn manufacturers; the garment manufacturers; and Level 4, the retailers, identifying the usage of colour forecasting information at the different production areas of the industry. Historically, the forecasting sector was incorporated within the manufacturing sector, until forecasting companies were established and relieved the primary market sector of the growing complexities of the forecasting process.

The responsibility for colour direction is now beginning to change as the current system of manufacturing and retailing is restructured. Many fashion manufacturing companies are producing garment designs and specifications around the table of their design room, along with the buyers of the top high street retail stores. Production of the garments is undertaken by CMT (cut, make and trim) factories, and the fashion company may then screen print the surface design onto the garments according to their clients' requirements. The specifications, including the colour range, are agreed by both parties and though the initial colours are determined by the retail sector, the fashion company advises on any technical problems they may encounter when working with particular colours on certain fabrics or fibres.

The system previously in operation has now changed in some areas of the industry. Retailers are becoming more aware of the consumer, observing and testing through in-store trials in order to anticipate more accurately preferences within their own market niche. They then dictate their requirements back to the manufacturing sector, thereby shifting the onus for colour direction. If only large retailing companies existed, then the responsibility for colour would be entirely with the retailers. At present both systems operate concurrently, as independent or sole trading shops do not have the clout to demand their requirements from the manufacturers. Instead, they use wholesalers who act as middlemen between retailer and manufacturer. This increases the cost of products to the independent retailer, disadvantaging them further. However, even independent stores operate some kind of forecasting method in their efforts to supply garments that their customers will want to buy. Some kind of decision-making process has to be used to make informed choices on colour for stock, unless garments are to be selected totally randomly, or intuitively. Even this apparently obscure process of selection must be based on some sort of identifiable methodology using thought, reasoning processes and decision-making.

We found that many dye houses are working on a commission basis, dyeing to customer specifications, usually supplying only the larger companies. Also, some yarn merchants buy stock without consideration of their customers' needs, on the assumption that the yarns will sell eventually. Such merchants are often driven by low price opportunities (stock clearance sales) more than by planned stock purchasing. These sales-driven rather than market-driven businesses are still supplying the independent retailers through manufacturers and wholesalers. But would it not make better business sense to stock to demand? Also, chances of repeat orders are hindered when the yarn eventually sells out some years later as it is then difficult to match the dyelot. Some companies appear not to carry out any kind of forecasting.

The current colour forecasting process

Colour forecasting aims to evaluate accurately the moods and buying behaviour of consumers; it collects colour data, analysing and interpreting it intuitively. The process depicts the possibilities and anticipates the direction of colour, as well as assessing the rate of change seasonally in order to establish what timing of such changes is acceptable to the consumer. The seasonal colour stories indicate hue, value and intensity and are heavily promoted throughout the industry. While these stories are thought important to the generation of high street sales, they can also set limitations, dissuading individual companies from using their intuition and feelings for colour direction based on their own sales data. However, those with knowledge of the process are reluctant to divulge any in-depth information either because of commercial secrecy or because they find it difficult to explain the system in detail.

The colour forecasting process involves the series of activities identified in Chapter 2, including data sourcing and collection; analysis and evaluation; interpretation and presentation. The many varied sources used by the colour forecaster create a database, which can be described as the input of the system, as shown in Figure 4.3.

The final result is referred to as the output of the system and can either be viewed as a colour story or as a trend prediction package. The stage between the input and output is that of transformation, i.e. what takes place in order to change the data from source into the final result. This transformation stage is essentially the process of colour forecasting as a tool for the application of seasonal trends for the fashion and textile industry. The first activity in the compilation of a colour story is collecting the data. Hard data is assessable and recorded, such as sweet wrappers and fabric samples; soft data remains in the forecaster's memory, employing aware-ness and observation skills. The information is then analysed using a process of assessment and elimination, employing

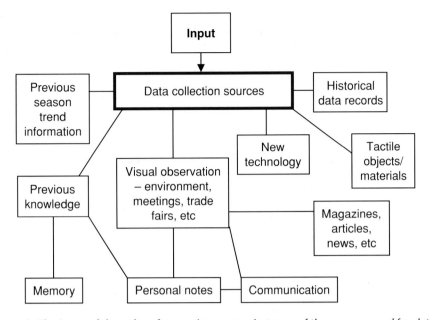

Figure 4.3 The input of the colour forecasting system in terms of the sources used for data collection.

intuitive skills as well as thought, decision and reasoning processes which we will term soft skills. The information is then interpreted, giving it meaning, using these same soft skills and so the colour story develops, via a process of assessment, comparison, selection, exploration and experimentation.

This development continues until the forecaster is satisfied with the result. The colour story is then refined through a process of elimination, again involving the soft skills. The current colour forecasting process anticipates consumer acceptability, with the forecaster accepting or rejecting certain colours. If colours are rejected then the process can begin again at any point, even as far back as collecting further data. If the colour story is accepted, then a final colour story is completed through to packaging for presentation. Predictions are then established through promotion and marketing. A model of the current colour forecasting process is shown in Figure 4.4.

This model was validated by testing a large sample of personnel within the manufacturing, retail and specialist sectors of the fashion and textile industry involved in forecasting. Over 80% agreed that the model was a close representation of the current colour forecasting process. The model was subsequently improved by taking into account feedback from the industry. Those using a different methodology were

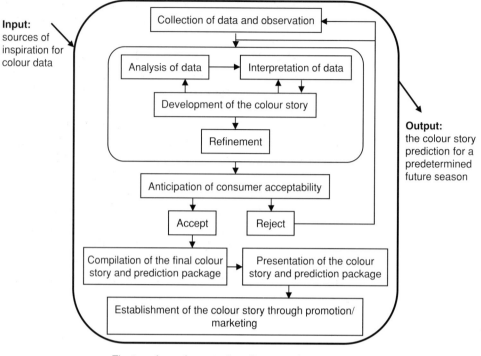

Input:
sources of
inspiration for
colour data

Output:
the colour story
prediction for a
predetermined
future season

Collection of data and observation

Analysis of data → Interpretation of data

Development of the colour story

Refinement

Anticipation of consumer acceptability

Accept   Reject

Compilation of the final colour story and prediction package

Presentation of the colour story and prediction package

Establishment of the colour story through promotion/ marketing

The transformation: a tool to allow manufacturers and retailers in the fashion and textile industry to provide products in consumer acceptable/desirable colours.

Figure 4.4 A model of the current colour forecasting process.

identified as independent retailers who claimed not to use a forecasting process.

Testing the model of the current forecasting process

The accuracy of any prediction is validated through sales on the high street and to test the effectiveness of the current colour forecasting process, we asked the general public their opinions. We found that only half were satisfied with the colour range available to them. Forecasters aim to satisfy 80% of the general public with their predictions but the current colour forecasting process is not providing the level of satisfaction needed by the manufacturing and retailing sectors of the industry. The process would benefit from some improvement to create more sales on the high street and offer more security for manufacturers. Feedback indicated that the colour choice is too narrow as most high street stores are promoting the same colour stories. On the whole, this survey indicated a high percentage of the general public would welcome a wider colour selection.

Eighty-three percent said that colour would or had influenced their purchase. Colour is a strong influence when purchasing fashion garments and sometimes the fabric, particularly specialist fabrics such as denim and suede, will influence a purchase. Also, style and fabric sometimes persuade the consumer to purchase even though an alternative colour would have been preferred. Staple or neutral colours (such as white, black, cream, beige) are more likely to be bought as a compromise to preferred colours than fashion colours would be. These staple colours are therefore considered by the industry as safe colours. Fashion colours or fad colours require more skill on the part of the forecasters to anticipate their level of acceptance and by which segment of the consumer market. It is the forecasting of these colours that would particularly benefit from an improved process.

The missing link

In Chapter 1 we identified the consumer as being one of the prime driving forces of fashion. Before the industrial revolution, designers had close professional relationships with their clients (those able to afford fashion) as shown in Figure 4.5. As

Pre-industrial revolution

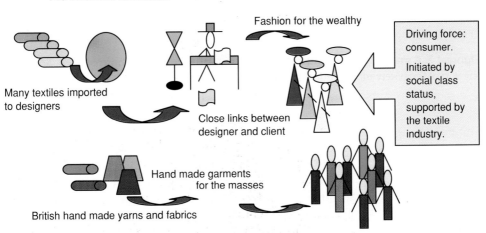

Fashion for the wealthy

Driving force: consumer.

Initiated by social class status, supported by the textile industry.

Many textiles imported to designers

Close links between designer and client

Hand made garments for the masses

British hand made yarns and fabrics

Figure 4.5 A snapshot of the fashion and textile industry prior to the industrial revolution.

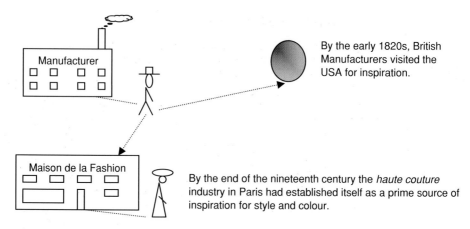

By the early 1820s, British Manufacturers visited the USA for inspiration.

By the end of the nineteenth century the *haute couture* industry in Paris had established itself as a prime source of inspiration for style and colour.

Figure 4.6 Early inspiration sources for the manufacturing industry.

Industrial revolution to the end of the nineteenth century

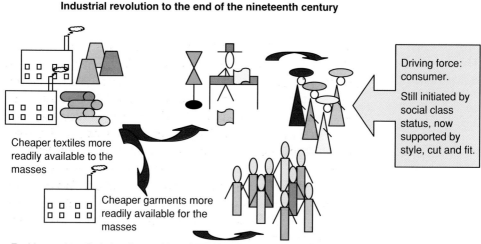

Driving force: consumer.

Still initiated by social class status, now supported by style, cut and fit.

Cheaper textiles more readily available to the masses

Cheaper garments more readily available for the masses

Fashion and textile industries working closer together

Figure 4.7 A snapshot of the fashion and textile industry during the industrial revolution to the end of the nineteenth century.

the textile industry thrived, new sources of inspiration were sought by manufacturers, demonstrating an early demand for forecasting, shown in Figure 4.6. While couture designers maintained their links with clients, the industry did not. This is illustrated in Figure 4.7.

By the twentieth century, direct links between consumers and designers were very few, only existing in the *haute couture*

Turn of the twentieth century

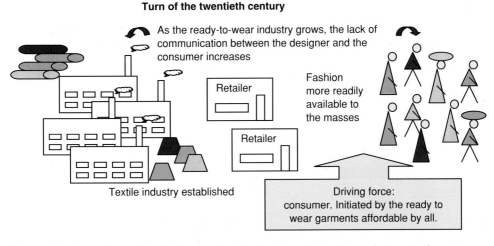

Figure 4.8 A snapshot of the fashion and textile industry during the early twentieth century.

industry (see Figure 4.8). As designers within the industry do not work on a one-to-one basis with clients, there is no direct link between the industry and the consumer. As this lack of communication increases, manufacturers become less informed of consumer needs. This became recognised and by 1930, a small number of forecasting companies were established in Britain following in the footsteps of the USA.

By the early 1930s seasonal colour palettes were emerging as an important directive for trend information. This development seemed to disappear over the subsequent 40 years, possibly with the demise of The British Colour Council, the originator of the concept.

The notion of fashion being consumer directed became increasingly evident and important. More forecasting companies were established during the 1960s and 1970s and marketing strategies became crucial for company survival. As the recession lifted, consumer lifestyles became ever more varied. Marketing techniques rose to this challenge and the industry's need for precise consumer colour trend information increased, particularly within the primary market sector – the fibre, yarn and fabric manufacturers.

Following the lead of the fashion company Next, colour established itself as a key marketing strategy and a more important driving force of fashion. Forty years after The British Colour Council initiated the seasonal colour it now took a key

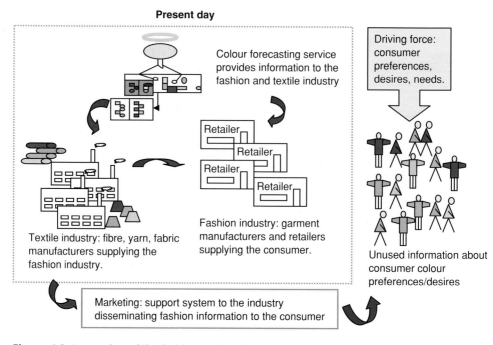

Present day

Colour forecasting service provides information to the fashion and textile industry

Driving force: consumer preferences, desires, needs.

Retailer

Retailer

Retailer

Retailer

Textile industry: fibre, yarn, fabric manufacturers supplying the fashion industry.

Fashion industry: garment manufacturers and retailers supplying the consumer.

Unused information about consumer colour preferences/desires

Marketing: support system to the industry disseminating fashion information to the consumer

Figure 4.9 A snapshot of the fashion and textile industry today.

role in forecasting. However, forecasters may still be guilty of influencing colour direction as opposed to anticipating it. Figure 4.9 presents a snapshot of the present state of the industry in relation to the consumer. Is consumer demand for colour really sought and recognised? Are the forecasters still assuming our demands and preferences? Or are they deliberately trying to direct them?

Judging by the end-of-season sales on the high street, consumers' needs are still not being met successfully. This may be due to the fact that observations of consumer desire reflect colours already available; one cannot observe the general public wearing colours not available to purchase.

While the driving force of fashion has always been the consumer, the economy of the industry also has a bearing upon fashion – or at least upon the rate of change of fashion. Due to the structure of production costs, colour is a relatively easily changeable factor. Colour has therefore become a very important element of the driving force as well as a powerful marketing aide. Sales have become heavily dependent upon seasonal colour stories and colour therefore plays a substantial role in the fashion and textile industry. The consumer

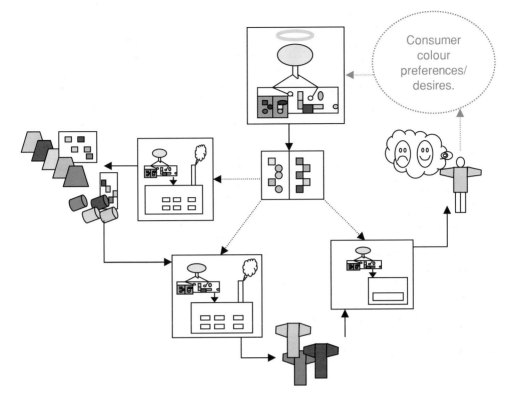

Figure 4.10 The missing link – consumer colour preference information.

influences the validation of colour forecast predictions, and is also a source of information through market research, though this area appears to still be relatively unexplored (see Figure 4.10).

Creating a better model for the colour forecasting process

Colour forecasting can be viewed both as a service and as a process. The service is the marketing function of the prediction packages, the product of the colour forecasting process. The process is used to produce and promote a selection of colours. The industry uses the prediction packages to assist in their colour decisions, in the hope that their resulting products will achieve optimum sales by meeting the desires, needs and preferences of the consumer.

Ideally, the consumer should benefit from the availability of desirably coloured products on the high street. The level of benefit here is the real crux of the matter under consideration and determines the effectiveness of the whole process. The higher the level of benefit for the consumer, the higher the volume of sales on the high street (subject to disposable income and state of the economy). The accuracy of anticipating the consumer's colour preferences or demands determines how beneficial the service is to the consumer and to the fashion and textile industry. However, beneficiaries of the colour forecasting process can also be seen as its victims if the efficiency of the system is in question, and forecasts prove false.

The industry buys the prediction packages from the specialist forecasting sector to achieve a high volume of sales directed by consumer satisfaction. To make sure that the colour range is acceptable – or better still, desirable – to the consumer, testing the market is clearly preferable to anticipating it.

We found that almost 70% of respondents involved with the colour forecasting process felt that the current system could or should be improved to benefit both the fashion and textile industry and the consumer. More than half questioned were from the retail sector, indicating that this sector is highly conscious of consumer satisfaction, having a more direct link with the consumer. Another reason may be the apparent shift in responsibility for colour direction, as previously discussed.

The improved process model

A proposed improved model for colour forecasting is shown in Figure 4.11. As consumer preference data gathered in the shops would be more accurate than what the current system offers, the colour palette as a whole should not, theoretically, be rejected as much as in the current model. Individual colours may be eliminated while developing the final colour palette. We can therefore exclude the accept and reject stages of the current model (shown in Figure 4.4), used to anticipate consumer acceptability, in favour of a stage of selection and elimination which would take place between the analysis and interpretation stages much earlier in the process, therefore saving time between the refinement of the colour story and its final compilation.

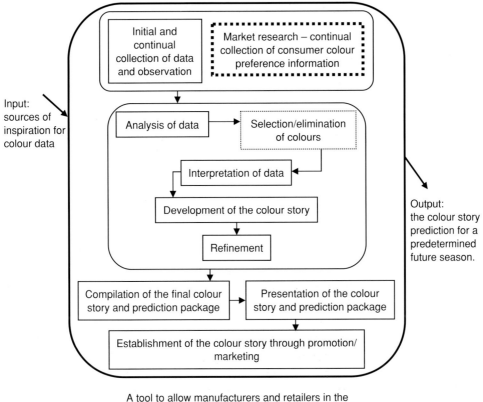

Input:
sources of
inspiration for
colour data

Output:
the colour story
prediction for a
predetermined
future season.

A tool to allow manufacturers and retailers in the
fashion and textile industry to provide products in
consumer desirable/acceptable colours

Figure 4.11 A proposed improved model for the colour forecasting process.

The proposed improved system would be used to collect, on a continual basis, data on colours not currently offered, as well as aiding assessment of the changing levels of acceptance of current colours offered on the high street. Alternatively, this could be a separate source of data incorporated into the input of the model if the information was collected and analysed by a third party, such as a market research consultancy. This could start another new sector, in the same way that the specialist forecasting sector was formed in the twentieth century. A device could be designed and sited in stores for consumers to interact with. The analysis from this would be undertaken by the designers and/or buyers currently using colour forecasting.

What forecasters said about the improved model

To validate this new model we asked the respondents for their views. Almost 70% of these in retailing agreed that their company would benefit from the improved system; almost 50% in manufacturing, and more than 80% of forecasters in the specialist sector also agreed. Those involved in the initial process would welcome a database of hard information to assist them develop their colour stories using stronger objective tools; the retailers would also appreciate this more tangible input. The manufacturers would find themselves more dictated to and become less proactive as the responsibility for colour direction changes.

This model does not suggest any need for consumers to understand the process of colour forecasting; they are simply asked to contribute to the data collection by indicating their colour preferences, or stating which colours are missing. It can be argued that consumers do not know what they want until they see it and marketing plays a key role to exposing them to something new in readiness for its acceptance. This theory can be incorporated into the improved model, as a series of colours would constantly be shown to those consumers interacting with the market research device.

There was slight concern by the industry that the methodology would no longer be forecasting if the consumers are given what they want. However, the colour palette to be tested has to be predicted initially and the testing stage would be used to verify its compilation.

A misconception of consumer preferences emerged from our survey. Some retailers give consideration to previous seasons' best sellers and see this as recognising consumer preferences. But as consumers can only buy what is available at the time, sales data gives no more than a snapshot of purchases in the present or past; it cannot indicate preferences for colours not currently on offer. In-store trials, where the general public is asked to give feedback on colour preferences, are used by some of the larger retailers though again obtaining feedback only on acceptability of selected colours. However, as this is a costly process it is not viable for the smaller retailers.

A comment of particular interest was made by personnel from the specialist sector that it is sometimes possible to base a season's new stock on a previous season's best sellers. While the range would not offer the consumer anything new in terms of colour, it would support the prime role of colour preference data and its application to the colour story. Though again, present colour preference data will not highlight potential new colours for the range.

One respondent commented that an element of surprise and beauty is always required of a range. Surely this element should be incorporated into the application of colour and the style of the end products. Also, we are not dismissing the importance of intuition, which will always exist. It should be remembered that colour is an important influential factor of the consumer's buying behaviour, but other aspects are also influential and important. It is the role of the designer and of the buyer to take these aspects into consideration. The garment as a whole should reflect something new, not the colour alone.

There was an encouragingly high level of positive feedback, including suggestions that using colour preference data could save a great deal of time for the system user. Consumer opinions were recognised as beneficial to the retail industry and including the consumer in the process was seen as sending out a positive message and making the consumer feel valued and respected. It was felt that consumer preference information would help to diminish the influence of the shop buyer's preferences in ranges. Many respondents believed the improved model was of interest and if achievable at speed, could supply the retail sector with suitably concise forecasts.

Other respondents were concerned that the proposed model could result in a rigid colour palette, unchanged from season to season. We do not consider this to be likely, as each retailer would be working with data obtained by their own customers, or potential customers. The information would therefore be unique to each store, producing different ranges in different stores, depending on the target market customer. This would result in more choice for the consumer along the high street as a whole. Retailers with more than one outlet would benefit from being able to regulate the different levels of colour acceptance in different store locations across the country – as well as across the world.

Some respondents felt the model was worth testing as it may lead to a return of style rivalry instead of the present price rivalry. Currently the consumer may benefit monetarily but at the expense of quality; in other words, you get what you pay for. Style rivalry however, stimulates quality at good value for money; this may be the key to the thriving manufacturing industry that the western world once had, making them strongly competitive once more.

There was positive feedback for the development of a method to capture consumer preference data quickly and to constantly monitor changes of taste. Marketing was highlighted as a possible way of enabling the consumer to continually influence colour ranges before products went on the shelves in the high street.

Retailers are becoming more aware of consumers' needs and desires through market segmentation and target market profiling developed to assist the retailer to stock in accordance with the requirements of their average customer. The target market customer profile is fictitious but is based upon market research, which includes demographical information and lifestyle analysis. The proposed new colour forecasting model would be highly beneficial to retailers, re-establishing the lost links with the consumer since the growth of the industry.

The missing link is that of consumer colour preference. The survey conducted in order to validate the current model and to test the proposed improved model with personnel within the industry suggested that a high percentage was in favour of improving the current colour forecasting system and in particular, that the inclusion of consumer colour preference data would be advantageous to the retail sector.

Summary

A process for forecasting colour has evolved and while this process may vary slightly from user to user (and some personnel appear to be unaware of using a system at all), the model of the current process discussed in this chapter is representative of how it works throughout the fashion and textile industry. However, just because a process is widely adopted does not mean it is working to its optimum level, nor that improvements or updates to the system should not be considered. In fact, fashion and consumer desire is an ever moving and changing energy so it does not make sense for the colour forecasting process to be stagnant in its approach to trend prediction.

As our survey showed, the current process is not attaining the level of satisfaction on the high street that forecasters aim for. We have looked at one way in which the present process could be improved. It is not suggested that this is the only way, nor that no other improvements could be identified, tested and applied. The development of trend prediction should be an ongoing process, like fashion itself. The recognition of the current shift of responsibility for the direction of colour within the industry demonstrates the need to remain sensitive to change.

In this chapter

We have discussed the current forecasting process in greater depth through models and looked at one way of improving the process for the benefit of both the industry and the consumer.

5 The colour forecaster's tool kit

We have already been introduced to the terminology used by the forecasters and are now better able to assess the value of writing and broadcasting on colour forecasting and the influence that the process has on the fashion and textile industry. Much of the industry has become dependent on forecasting services, despite there being little understanding of the processes involved. It also has to be said, that what is reported in the media does not contribute to any understanding.

For a subjective concept to be widely accepted and considered, a substantial amount of theoretical background is required. The subjective side of colour forecasting needs to be better understood, modelled and tested for it to survive the transition from the hypothetical world to that of empirical reality.

We will now examine more closely the tools of colour forecasting, referring back to the model of the current forecasting process discussed in Chapter 4, and also discuss their subsequent application within the process. This will help us to further demystify the subjective tools.

In this chapter

We shall discuss and understand the more subjective tools in the colour forecasting process. We will learn more about the individual components of the process, including their strengths and weaknesses. Important soft tools include: intuition, inspiration and thought, reasoning and decision-making.

Understanding the tools of the forecaster

As previously discussed (see Chapter 2), the colour forecaster's tool kit comprises both subjective, art-based, or soft tools; and the more objective and scientifically-based hard tools.

The soft tools available to the forecaster include awareness and observation, both empirical tools grounded in experimentation and previous knowledge. More ambiguous but as fundamental are tools commonly known as intuition and inspiration. Because soft tools are essentially internal functions, operating within the mind, it is difficult to measure, analyse or evaluate them; they can only be described in subjective terms.

The hard tools include statistical analysis and conceptual models derived from previous trend information, sales data, and a range of analytic programmes available as computer software. Inspiration can be drawn from these and incorporated effectively into the development and marketing of the colour story.

Both hard and soft tools are used in the first stage of the forecasting process – data collection. The sources used by the forecasters to collect this data have been identified in Chapter 4 as the input aspect of the process. Sourcing and data collection are usually interpreted as one function but we will discuss them separately here as they represent two distinct components of the system, with differing complexities.

Sourcing data (input)

There is an infinite quantity of sources available to the forecaster for inspiration and colour data collection and again, sources divide into those of a subjective nature and those considered to be more objective.

Subjective sources are many and varied and their nature is subjective because the information is usually not recorded and therefore unavailable for others to use. It remains in the possession of the forecaster, held in the memory. This information comes to the forecaster through their awareness and observation skills which can be exercised at any time of the day or night and in any location. Because the forecaster constantly uses these skills, whether consciously or not, the process of data collection is a continuous one. Events where these skills would be put to particularly good use include shopping trips, visiting other parts of the country or trips abroad, watching television, films and theatre. Also being in pubs and clubs, at pop concerts and parties, and even on the street – in fact wherever and whenever forecasters are out the office or studio, they will be constantly observing their surroundings: the environment, the people and also the moods or emotions. All this is directed to the memory and retained, though personal notes may be kept, making the evidence more objective. Simply talking and more importantly, listening to people, their opinions, lifestyle, behaviour and observing their body language will give forecasters vital information. Unless this information is recorded in some way by the forecaster, the data remains subjective and intangible.

Previous knowledge is another useful source of information as the process of sourcing and collection of data is a continual one. Colours previously identified and rejected by the forecaster when compiling the previous season's colour range may now be a potentially acceptable colour for the new colour range. Also, as the direction of colour change is gradual, the forecaster must always be aware of previous trend prediction colour ranges and the colours the general public are wearing today in order to follow through the direction of change and assess the rate of change.

Objective sources available to the forecaster include previous seasons' trend information, either their own company's or those of others. Newspaper articles and magazines provide a rich source of ideas and inspiration, as do historical archives of colour and fashion such as museums, art galleries, libraries and fashion books, old magazines, and dressmaking and knitting patterns. Tactile objects and materials can be collected anywhere in the world, from your own home and garden to street markets, forests and beaches.

Other major sources for the forecaster are the trade fairs and colour meetings, though information from these is generally filtered and delivers a precise proposed colour story, already agreed upon. Forecasters also keep abreast of new technology, for example if a fibre company were developing metallic yarns, forecasters may consider these colours and textures as a major theme, being aware of the company's need to promote its new products.

Thus we can see there are many sources to which the forecaster can go for a diverse range of data. However, there is more to it than simply being there and the data needs to be collected for it to be used.

Data collection

In Chapter 4 we identified the sources of data used by forecasters and termed it the input of the process, as demonstrated in the models. As previously mentioned, data may be described as objective or hard data, or as subjective or soft. Hard data is visible to all, such as samples of fabric, paper, leaves, photographs, etc. Soft data is contained within the memory of the individual and therefore not accessible by anyone else. It is preferable for the forecaster to have hard data for precise colour interpretation and accurate reproduction as the memory is not reliable.

Data can be collected using three basic approaches: verbal; visual; using the other senses or emotional. Verbal interpretation involves asking for information, a simple tool found to be lacking in the current forecasting process. We suggested that asking the general public their opinions of colour to reveal their preferences would possibly improve the current system by providing a database of colour acceptability for relevant niche markets that would be of benefit to both the industry and the consumer. Other verbal interpretations would involve the forecaster prompting and listening to people's opinions and reactions to colour. Results of these communications could be recorded as hard data or simply remembered as soft data. This type of data collection appears to be little used by the forecasters at any level, from the initial forecasters to the retailers. The retailers are in a good position to use the consumer as a source of information, by simply talking to people on the shop floor, or by setting up a more formal data collection system. The information should then be fed back into the colour forecasting process as discussed in Chapter 4, through an improved process model. It is possible that there are independent retailers already employing this type of data collection, as they are most likely to have stronger links with their customers than do the high street store sales assistants. The owner of an independent store has a vested interest in the profitability and survival of their business, whereas employees of the multiple retailers do not have this vested interest and are less likely to be so attentive to the consumer. Even if those employees do chat freely to customers and have insight into their likes and dislikes, it is very unlikely that this information is passed on, even to store managers, let alone back to the company's designers and buyers. Retailers could benefit greatly by training their staff to extract this type of information to be formally reported, or even better, to develop some sort of in-store interactive system for the consumer to use.

The second method of data collection is by visual interpretation. This utilises the colour forecasting tools of observation and awareness. The information is recorded, analysed and evaluated and may be taken from an individual or from groups of individuals. This is the prime method of data collection currently used by colour forecasters. Observation and awareness techniques are generally employed covertly so that people are unaware of being watched and included as a source of information.

The process of observation is complex as it incorporates the soft tools of sensation and perception. Sensation may be viewed as a function of the senses, a rousing of the emotions, whereas perception is a more intuitive activity within the mind. Three types of observation have been identified: casual, systematic and participant. Casual observation is like awareness, becoming conscious of moods and trends through casual observation and sensing. Employing systematic observation however, the forecaster is more aware of patterns forming based upon the casual observations first made. At this stage the forecaster consciously looks for more evidence to support the data already acquired through awareness and observation, though not at the expense of further casual observation. Participant observation is when the observer experiences through hands-on activities. Forecasters may do this when shopping for themselves and being aware that they too are consumers and thinking as a consumer would while selecting items to purchase. Through this experience the forecaster would be made aware of colours that they personally feel are missing or desirable. This type of observation is the third type of data collection and employs the senses and emotional interpretation. Forecasters can deliberately put themselves in the position of the consumer to assess and evaluate the colours available or potentially available in future seasons but the responses will be their own. In order to have insight into the thoughts and feelings of the individual consumers, the information needs to be taken directly from them, otherwise it is merely presumption. This reasoning supports the improved model discussed in Chapter 4.

It is questionable whether forecasters are consciously inclined to include into their predictions colours based upon their own preferences. Could the novice forecaster be more prone to doing this than the experienced one? Again, data of colour acceptability should take precedence over anticipating the results.

Colour forecasters use a process known as naturalistic observation when observing people in their everyday environment. Authors writing on this subject acknowledge its use for observing what is happening at a given time but also that this is not an ideal methodology for understanding why, in terms of thought, reasoning and decision-making processes. During naturalistic observation, the observer has no control over the process or outcome, therefore the results are more accurate than those of guesswork. If forecasters were knowledgeable about why consumers prefer particular colours by understanding the thought, reasoning and decision-making, this would be of benefit for future trend prediction formulation, particularly in relation to direction and rate of change.

There are two further tools of great importance to data collection that are also used throughout the entire colour forecasting process: intuition and inspiration.

Intuition

Intuition is one of the most important tools available to the forecaster, as we established in Chapter 2. In order to evaluate intuition in more detail, we now examine its underlying aspects and approach the subject from a wider perspective in order to place it in both its theoretical and empirical contexts.

The importance of intuition has long been recognised by philosophers of the past, so why does it now appear to have been swept under the carpet? – or has it? Is it more a case of using it unknowingly? Or using it but being unable to explain it and therefore underestimating its importance and value?

While some may recognise the existence of intuition and its role in the practicalities of today's objective world, many still dismiss it. However, there is a minority that appreciates the necessity to bridge the gap between the intuitive and objective worlds. This could open up a new, rich and diverse field of research leading to a better appreciation of the subjective attributes of the human mind.

While scientific methodologies do not acknowledge intuition, there have been distinguished scientists willing to recognise the value and importance of intuition. Particular emphasis has been made to its role in discovery, an argument for its indispensability in science. The modern-day physicist and author, Fritjof Capra refers to intuition as being the insight and creativity that is required in scientific research in order to break new ground. He recognised that this process tends to occur when the mind is in a relaxed state as opposed to being applied consciously to find a solution. Einstein was also reputed to have acknowledged the value of intuition to the application of problem solving. This was evident as early as 1905 in his PhD thesis and early papers, which formed the basis of the theory of relativity, published in full in 1916.

Colour forecasting can be viewed as a problem to solve, or as a challenge in terms of compiling a colour range that will be acceptable to the consumer for a predetermined season in the near future, where the final colour story is the solution. Colour forecasters would not necessarily view this as a problem but possibly a challenge, and most definitely as being their job. In scientific terms it is a problem; for the creative it is an opportunity.

Intuition is more widely recognised in the art disciplines than in the scientific ones. It is often thought of as synonymous to the artist's instinct to know when something is right, such as a painter's colour or a composer's melody. The important factor is that in the art world there is no need for justification, whereas in the world of science, everything must be verified, tested and measured. If intuition is not quantified, at least enough to understand it, it has no apparent place in science. Intuition however, could be interpreted as the driving force of creativity, which can inspire the pursuit of new knowledge.

Applying this to colour forecasting, forecasters are in a sense obliged to justify the trends predicted, at least to their clients. However, the reasoning can be cleverly interpreted through marketing to convince the client of its legitimacy. The real thought, reasoning and decision-making processes are not clear and do not explain how the forecaster decides what is right and what is not, nor when and how the final colour story has been achieved. This is the intuitive element of colour forecasting.

While the scientific world generally neglects the subject of intuition, it does appear to have a role in behavioural research, with many authors writing specifically on thinking and thought modelling, apparently more open to the concept of intuition and its usefulness. Decision-making is a process of judgement and elimination based upon cognitive thought, reasoning and intuition.

Some forecasters have expressed a fear that if intuition was quantified, it would limit its creative potential, at least in the minds of those made aware of its definition. On the other hand, they may be equally fearful, or more so, if information users took full control of the forecasting process rendering their services dispensable. There is an element of freedom of choice for the information user to implement their own intuition beyond the advice of the forecasters. In this way, information users could exercise their own forecasting methodology which would be a more cost effective and more accurate means of that company's merchandise meeting consumer demand. This highlights, yet again, the importance of prediction within the manufacturing sector.

Inspiration

Inspiration is usually considered to have a more spiritual connotation, as ideas seem to appear just at the right time, apparently coming from nowhere and are noted to be remarkably accurate. This is often referred to as the 'Eureka Factor', but where does it come from? There are two identifiable origins, the first being the many sources available to the forecaster that provide a visual and tangible aspect from where inspiration can be derived. These sources may provoke thoughts, feelings and intuitive hunches. Inspiration can also come from sound, the spoken word or possibly more subjectively from music, animal noises, etc. The second, and possibly the most controversial source of inspiration is when these seemingly appropriate and timely notions come to mind out of the blue. These notions are characteristically detached from any visual stimulant or conscious thought. Where this inspiration comes from is difficult for many to contemplate and for those who do have a notion of their origin and are able to explain this, providing proof is far from easy, leaving the whole subject open to speculation.

There is, however, the hypothesis of the universal mind. Whilst too obscure a concept for some, for those with a more open and creative mind, it is a possibility that has recently become a subject of research. The argument of biologist Dr Rupert Sheldrake – one such researcher who is not ignoring the importance of genetics – is based on the hypothesis that our genetic programme is stored outside the body as opposed to inside it by deoxyribonucleic acid (DNA). DNA is a record of the physical body's data only. The term morphogenetics has been given to the theory which is concerned with the body's spiritual make up. Sheldrake believes that this source of information can be tapped in order to acquire new knowledge and skills. Successful experiments can substantiate this claim. The theory puts forward the idea that memory is stored within the morphogenetic fields as opposed to within the brain. This is said to be akin to the universal mind that the clairvoyant and telepathist can tap into.

The eminent psychic Edgar Cayce popularised, if not founded, the concept of the Akashic record, the Sanskrit word for 'etheric matter of the universe'. This is thought to be accessible to us all, if we know how to use it. When inspiration appears to come from nowhere, we have possibly unconsciously accessed this universal knowledge.

Some argue that inspiration and intuition are messages conveyed to us from the spirit world, a sort of go-between who accesses the information on our behalf then plants the seed of thought into our minds. Another viewpoint extends Sheldrake's theory, incorporating the universal law of 'like attracts like'. In essence those of a particular psychological make up will be drawn towards using certain types of information. Not all will have enough energy to put this information to good use, hence instances of people having ideas and not seeing them through only to have someone else with the same idea bring it to fruition. This happened frequently during the 1800s with the development of the sewing machine when the same or very similar ideas appeared concurrently on either side of the Atlantic, creating fury and frustration for many inventors not having the financial backing to patent their ideas, let alone to market them.

The similarities evident in colour stories shown by many members in attendance at various colour meetings suggest that such a universal mind could exist. Is it possible that a forecaster's intuition really does tap into the spirit of the time? And if so, can this claim ever be proved?

The 'Age of Aquarius' is the term given to the astrological zodiac phase that began in 2000 and will last until the year 4000. It is proclaimed to be a period of foresight and innovation with particular emphasis upon science, technology, psychology and rationalism; characteristics directly attributed to the zodiac sign Aquarius. As its presence is being felt through the rise of the ecology movement and more people become actively and more openly involved in the utopian vision of New Age thinking, more research may be encouraged to shed light on this subject, backed up by more concrete evidence. In the mean time, each of us must decide for ourself what inspiration and intuition mean to us and where we think it comes from.

Processing the data and applying the colour forecasting process

The subsequent stages of the colour forecasting process involve the series of tools identified and modelled in Chapter 4. The section of the model we are now referring to is shown in Figure 5.1.

Analysis and interpretation

At some point, either after data collection is complete or once sufficient information has been gathered and can be collated for use but while collection is still in progress, the information is analysed. The process of analysis separates elements and identifies any specific classifications or patterns in order for data to be arranged in a meaningful manner. The resulting meaning is recognised as the interpretation process and this explains why the patterns or groups are as they are. In other words, the formulation of the colour story begins.

The initial information gathered will determine the basis, theme or mood of the colour story. Data collection becomes more directed as the theme is established and further defined.

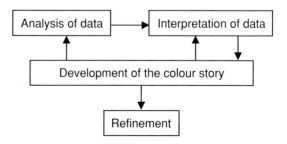

Figure 5.1 The first stages of the current colour forecasting model used for colour story development.

A stage is then reached when additional information is less important than the analysis of what has already been collected. That is to say that the information collected takes a more significant role as supporting evidence for the proposed colour story than of promoting inspiration. Thought, reasoning and decision-making become the driving forces behind the ideas towards accomplishing the colour story.

The development of the colour story

Once the information has been analysed and interpreted, it is evaluated. This may involve scientific measurement but usually for colour forecasting a more intuitive judgement is used. This process is a key element in the development of the colour story when the forecaster experiments with the data, organising it for visual impact and employing thought, reasoning and decision-making, as well as intuition to eliminate, reorganise and add further data. The elimination element involves a process of accepting or rejecting pieces of data. Due recognition should be given to creativity as one of the key elements responsible for discovery, resulting from this analysis stage.

Refinement

Finally the colour story is refined, this may involve some 'tweaking', adding or taking away of small pieces of data or simply rearranging it for better effect. At this stage, the layout of the final presentation of the colour story will usually have been decided and probably been set out in draft but not yet fixed, enabling refinement to take place.

Assessment and completion

At this point, the final elements of the colour forecasting process are undertaken to complete the colour range and present the colour story either to clients or to colleagues. We can see this stage of the current model in Figure 5.2.

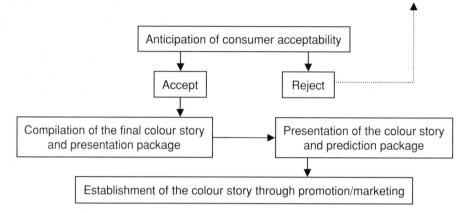

Figure 5.2 The final stages of the current colour forecasting model for final colour story compilation and presentation.

Anticipation

The next stage of the colour forecasting process is anticipating the consumer's or client's acceptance of the colour story as it stands at this moment in time. How much the forecaster actually considers the acceptability of the colours by the consumer is unsure. They certainly assess whether or not they feel that their clients and potential clients are going to be inspired by the colour story and particularly by its final presentation, as this influences sales of the prediction packages. Likewise, fashion and textile students producing mood boards as part of their course assignments would do well to assess not just how closely the brief has been adhered to, but also the level of acceptance or desirability it offers the person who will be marking the work. The final result should be attractive and inspiring; this is of particular value to the final presentation of work and will be discussed in Chapter 6.

The models described in Chapter 4 suggest that the anticipation process is separate and follows on from the developmental stages and that parts or all of the colour story could be rejected at this stage. We must point out that firstly, the anticipation, accept and reject stages will be iterative processes undertaken throughout the developmental stages. In reality, the members of the industry surveyed did not criticise this and agreed that this stage is indeed in the correct position in the current colour forecasting model. Though we appreciate that the nature of the process is so compact and integrated that there is often an overlap of the processes and that the model is only a representation of the process made simple. Also it is very unlikely – though not impossible – that a professional would reject the entire colour story at this stage, particularly as the forecaster develops an understanding of colour and of the colour forecasting process through experience. Students on the other hand, may feel disappointed with their attempts and will start all over again if there is enough time.

The forecasters may however reject ideas for the final packaging at this stage, in favour of perhaps something more eye-catching and novel to set them apart from the competition, or for something more in keeping with the company's image and style.

Compilation, presentation and establishment

The last stages of the colour forecasting process include the compilation of the final colour story, the presentation of the data and finally convincing clients of its validity. The compilation may in fact again be an integral part of the developmental stages. The presentation can refer to either the visual aspects or the delivery of the final packaging to clients or both. The delivery is also part of the establishment process using marketing techniques. We have already discussed how colour stories are promoted through trade fairs and exhibitions in Chapter 2, and how they are established through promotion and marketing. The compilation and presentation stages will be further discussed in Chapter 6.

Thought, reasoning and decision-making processes

With a better understanding of the process of colour forecasting, we come to realise that throughout all its stages, the forecaster employs the soft tools of intuition, thought, reasoning and decision-making.

Theoretically, pure intuition or a totally random selection could be employed to produce a colour palette for forecasting. The success of the selection could be tested either through market research or through observing sales on the high street. This would of course be subject to trial and error which would take too long and not be financially viable.

Through Chapter 4 we developed a sound understanding of how the process of colour forecasting is achieved as a whole, but so far we have lacked an appreciation of why particular choices of colour are made and what influences the rate and direction of change. In other words, what the thought, reasoning and decision-making processes are. Authors on this subject agree that knowledge either previously attained or since acquired from the environment has a particular bearing upon the thought, reasoning and decision-making processes and that memory and visual sources of data are important assets. The importance of perception has also been acknowledged in these processes.

Perception is the understanding of data obtained through the various modes of observation and sensation. Experience also effects the perception of a concept, either supporting or contradicting the original point of view. If prior experience is the main influential factor for how data is perceived or understood, this is known as idiosyncratic perception. When the majority of the observers or forecasters come to similar conclusions, this general perception may be referred to as a universal perception. This occurs when similarities are identified at initial colour meetings and relates to the universal mind concept discussed earlier.

A series of steps is identifiable when given the brief to develop a colour story and with each step, a change occurs in the forecaster's level of knowledge. Additional knowledge depends on the brief, such as the requirements for a particular company. Steps taken thereafter, in terms of the collection of information and the thought, reasoning and decision-making processes change the raw data into a colour story. The forecaster uses the process identified in the model until a satisfactory colour story has been developed resulting in a trend prediction package for the initial forecasters or a product range for the designers and buyers of the industry.

An interesting point to ponder here is: How does one know when the final colour story has been achieved? The colour forecaster appears to base this decision upon previous knowledge and on intuition.

It is important to remember that it is not only the forecaster who uses decision-making but also the information users, e.g. individual company designers. The designer's role in the prediction procedure is of much importance as a selection process to decide the colours that will be used for the end product and offered to the consumer. It would be interesting to establish therefore, if the same thought, reasoning and decision-making are used by both the forecaster and the information users, who are currently forecasting trends for their company's products. Is it fair to assume that the information users are confined by the colour stories presented by the forecasters? Or do they exercise their own powers of prediction?

Summary

The industry will benefit from a better understanding of the soft tools used in colour forecasting, both to give the process more credibility and to demystify it. This will help to establish the importance of colour forecasting and dispel any negative attitudes towards it.

Although specific stages of the process can be identified, we must appreciate that these can overlap due to the complex nature of the colour forecasting process and also that each stage incorporates elements of experimentation. This adds to the body of knowledge held by the forecaster, and intuition and thought, reasoning and decision-making are used throughout, making them an integral part of both the process as a whole, and of each individual component.

In this chapter

We have considered the concept of the empirical and theoretical worlds to understand the difference between the subjective and objective sides of colour forecasting. Various methodologies (the tool kit) available for data collection were discussed and evaluated and finally intuition, a vital soft tool of the colour forecasting process, was analysed to establish a deeper understanding. This led to the recognition of the importance of decision-making, thought and reasoning in forecasting.

The problem for the student or novice colour forecaster is knowing how to tell when a satisfactory result has been achieved. To help shed light on this, the soft tools are further investigated through the development of colour stories in the following chapter. We will also learn more the about the complexities of thought, reasoning and decision-making processes, as well as appreciate and develop high standards of presentation through the specially designed colour story and mood board workshop activity.

6 Colour story development and presentation

Through the previous chapters we have developed a deeper understanding of the tools that colour forecasters use. We will now look further at the application of the colour forecasting process to the development of colour stories. We have established that problems are encountered by the novice trying to understand the working of this process, as colour forecasters appear to be reluctant to divulge detailed information. This may in turn affect the quality of the teaching of the subject, reducing learning opportunities for the new forecaster. It is important for fashion and textile design students to understand the implications of colour and to know how to develop and work with colour trend information. Having gained a deeper appreciation of the colour forecasting process, we can now concentrate on the development of the colour story, mood boards and presentation skills. These aspects are fundamental to colour forecasting and an important part of design modules for students.

Just as there is a current lack of in-depth information on colour forecasting, there is also a shortage of descriptions of the development of mood boards, even though these are widely used by design students and throughout the industry. As with many creative subject areas, there are no hard and fast rules but there are some useful guidelines that students will benefit from understanding and following.

Before examining the development of colour stories in depth, we shall first look at how colour forecasting or trend prediction is taught and then used by student designers to produce colour stories. Students will benefit greatly from this as well as from the workshop approach designed to develop understanding, to enhance skills and to encourage creativity in colour story and mood board design and presentation, while developing a trend prediction portfolio.

In this chapter

We shall examine, discuss and experiment with:

- thought, reasoning and decision-making processes and the application of these to the current colour forecasting process
- the teaching of trend prediction modules on design courses
- the interpretation of trend information approaches to mood board and colour range development
- production and evaluation of trend information and mood board design
- examples of colour mood boards demonstrating high standards of presentation.

Studying trend prediction

Colour and fashion forecasters generally have fashion, textile or marketing related backgrounds. Students in these areas could work in the specialist sector or with the forecasting process in the role of a designer or buyer. Trend prediction may or may not be taught as a separate module; however, the majority of fashion and textile design related courses will encourage the development of skills necessary for compiling colour and style ranges. This is generally undertaken through the use of mood boards and sketchbooks, and the presentation of a final portfolio for assessment. These are a fundamental part of the colour forecasting process, incorporating the skills forecasters acquire and apply to their job.

Colour forecasting is not taught in isolation but often as part of a general trend prediction module. The aim of such modules will be to enable students to understand the role of the forecasting profession within the fashion and textile industry and to understand how colour prediction packages are developed. Current and past trend information may be evaluated in order to develop an understanding of prediction information and its role in the industry. This activity is usually part of the students' self-directed learning programme and found to be little understood or used by students. As it is an important part of the forecasters' role, we will develop techniques to identify, analyse and evaluate colour evolution, direction of change and rate of change. We will also learn to identify the moods conveyed by colour stories and to identify staple and fashion colours in a range through a worked example.

Identifying colour moods

The moods that individuals feel intuitively and sense from visual stimuli are subjective and stem from the individual's experiences and perceptions. A colour range may therefore instill a variety of moods within a group of individuals.

Figure 6.1 shows two sets of complete colour prediction ranges compiled by the authors, the first is an autumn/winter palette, the second a spring/summer one. Looking at the two sets of colours, we can see similarities between them because they are predictions for consecutive seasons. What you are interpreting is the colour evolution.

Look now at the autumn/winter palette as a whole: Do you think the colours appear light or heavy? Does the palette look harmonious or discordant? Do you think the palette has an overall warm feel or cool feel? Remember, at this stage we are considering the colour range as a whole and assessing our own emotions. Is the colour range predominantly clear, tonal (grey) or washed out? Are there large amounts of achromatics (black, white, grey) or neutral colours? Is there a dominance by one or two particular hues? It may help to squint a little when viewing the palette to help eliminate less dominant aspects.

The autumn/winter palette is in our opinion, due to many darks, predominantly rich and relatively harmonious, with perhaps a slightly more warm appearance. The palette is bright and clear in the main, with few achromatics or neutrals. There tends to be a dominance of blues ranging from blue/greens to violets and red/violets with a blue bias. The overall effect could be described as rich with a classy feel due to the dominance of blue.

Let us now consider the spring/summer palette. There is still a dominance of dark, rich colours, particularly orange shades. The palette as a whole is quite jarring on the eyes, especially the red/violets, like magenta; therefore the energy of this palette is more discordant or contrasting. The overall feel is still relatively warm though cool contrasts are evident. Colours

Autumn/winter

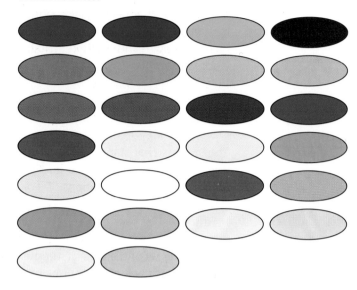

Spring/summer

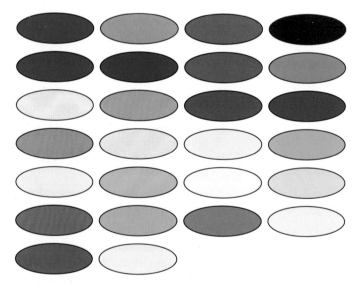

Figure 6.1 Autumn/winter and spring/summer trend prediction colour ranges.

are mostly bright and clear. The dominance of oranges conveys a warm, friendly feel that is inviting, and this is strongly contrasted by a higher energy feel of the red/violets.

You may disagree with some or all of this analysis but this does not mean either of us is wrong; we are all individuals with differing personalities, ideals, experiences and perceptions, enabling us all to interpret information to suit ourselves. If you are experiencing difficulties evaluating colour ranges, we suggest you look back at the colour wheel (p. 54) and colour knowledge (p. 52) to help you. There is a range of books available and listed in the Bibliography on p. 161 (e.g. Whelan's *Colour Harmony 2*) that provides aides for students evaluating colour moods. The examples worked through here refer to the colour palette as a whole. The 26 colours of both the autumn/winter palette and of the spring/summer palette were originally split into four themes for each season, using seven or eight colours for each theme. If the moods for each theme were evaluated, the results would be different for each and different again to the whole colour palette for each season.

Identifying staple and fashion colours

Staple colours are generally considered to be dark blues, greens and reds, black, white and light neutral colours, such as cream or beige and browns: these often seem to dominate the colour palette. Still referring to Figure 6.1, the staple colours of the autumn/winter palette are those with a dominant blue content, but also having a rich appearance, plus black and white. The fashion colours are less likely to appear in many subsequent or follow-on trends, as the acceptance by the consumer will be anticipated to be relatively brief. Some colours will be considered to have a very short acceptance period (possibly just one season) and are called fad colours. The fashion or fad colours of our autumn/winter palette the bright magentas, turquoise/blues and lime. These colours are more up-beat and jazzy than the remaining fashion colours of the palette, which have more classical attributes. The classical colours will be anticipated to be acceptable for longer than the fad ones.

The staple colours of our autumn/winter palette are present in the spring/summer palette but diminishing in favour of complementary orange shades, or browns; black remains but not white. The classic fashion colours are also diminishing, though the fad colours of the autumn/winter palette are to be seen for the spring/summer season.

Assessing colour evolution

The direction of colour change from the two palettes in Figure 6.1 demonstrates how the fashion colours have remained while the staple colours move away from the rich, dark blue spectrum to the rich shades of its complementary colour, orange (browns). This move will now allow for a shift in the fashion colours of follow-on predictions to produce a renewed and fresh colour palette. The classical fashion colours are diminishing but still present, and linking the staple and fashion colours are the softer beiges, mints, pale blues, yellows and pinks. Therefore, when assessing the moods, we can appreciate that the richness remains but the classical attribute is becoming more emphasised; with this, the palette has become more discordant, emphasising the flow of energy.

To assess the rate of these changes, a larger sample of follow-on trends would be required; it may take only a few seasons for some colours to change, whereas others may appear only for one season. When one or two particular colours appear in only one or two consecutive trend packages, there may be a genuine feeling that those particular colours may only be accepted for one or two seasons. However, there is the possibility of an error of judgement on the forecaster's part when compiling a trend, therefore those colours are not followed on in subsequent packages. Another possibility is that one or two colours may be included as tasters, to whet the information user's appetite for the colour before heavily promoting it in future trends. These misplaced colours may therefore be referred to as rogue colours or taster colours.

Workshop activity

Look at trend prediction packages in your library. Select one company's packages for at least four consecutive seasons. See if you can identify the moods, staple and fashion colours of each season, then assess the evolution of the colours by determining the direction and rate of colour change. This activity could be developed into a full-scale investigation for a major project.

Trend prediction modules

Researching and developing a prediction package for a chosen market is also part of the forecaster's job, which requires the development of personal creativity and high level presentation skills. In the main, modules are taught by one member of staff, though sometimes a guest lecturer may be invited to offer insights into the industry's perspective. The modules tend to be short, running over only one semester, preventing students from developing an initial database of information and hindering the data sourcing, collection and research stage, including all the relevant skills required.

The subject of forecasting colour and/or style may only warrant a short module and accorded relatively low weighting on fashion and design courses. However, the principles involved in producing colour and style ranges and theme or mood board development (including fabric sampling for design, fashion illustration and the development of presentation skills) are all a fundamental part of many design modules, whether fashion or textile related. Trend prediction therefore could be usefully included on other design modules. Skills developed would include colour knowledge (for colour reproduction using a variety of media and colour range development) and the practicalities of storyboard development, i.e. cutting, mounting, experimenting with different tools and materials, and fashion drawing. Craft related subjects like paper-making, painting effects and hand dyeing, would all be worth including in a specialist trend prediction module.

Modules are invariably run to a tight schedule and a large project assignment may be required. Small classes can be advantageous, as productive discussion workshops are possible that imitate what goes on at the colour meetings that forecasters attend. Individual tutorials enable the continuation of the practical work within the studio time but should not exclude the brainstorming sessions. Brainstorming is an inspirational exercise undertaken even after ideas have been formulated. The colour meetings that forecasters attend are in themselves a form of brainstorming, though at this stage there is more focus on identifying and collating patterns and similarities in the colours and moods presented by the members. Brainstorming is important in generating inspiration for ideas and solutions to problems where innovative and creative problem-solving can result.

Another significant skill to develop is time management – meeting deadlines at regular intervals aids the progression of a task. It is an extremely important element of not just the forecasting process in any sector but practically all roles in the fashion and textile industry, as deadlines must be met for the continuation of fashion and its survival as an industry.

Brainstorming sessions and constructive discussions are important for reviewing progress as well as addressing problems. Progress is a positive aspect whereas problems are negative. However, if problems are approached as challenges, they lose the negative elements that make them difficult to overcome. Problems encountered can be many and varied and discussing these obstacles is an excellent way of finding solutions to actual and potential problems. Many individuals find teamwork difficult but it is very much used in this industry where communication is key. Sometimes ideas are kept secret during the developmental stages to prevent competitors from stealing them. This is particularly evident in the fashion and textile industry, though when working in teams, it is important for all members to be aware of all the ideas and expect and accept sharing of the credit.

Trend prediction modules are mainly experimental and creative in nature with a very limited input of information other than the brief, or the module handbook. These modules tend to help individuals develop certain skills but do not actually teach the forecasting process. This may be partly because the process is poorly understood outside the profession and there is little information available. Ideally modules should be a balance of teaching the process in detail and promoting awareness of what is currently going on in the industry, our immediate environment and globally, alongside the development of creativity and of presentation skills. Computer aided design (CAD) tuition is a valuable part of the module, particularly developing skills with software packages such as PhotoShop, currently used in the trend prediction sector of the industry. The inclusion of colour knowledge here is not just desirable but essential.

We found that assignments and assessments of many trend prediction modules do not demonstrate the students' understanding of the forecasting process and that vitally important forecasting tools are not taught in detail or developed. Theoretically, anyone can produce a colour palette or range of colours without using any of the forecasting tools, by selecting colours intuitively for example. As long as the supporting evidence is supplied and presented well, the student can achieve a relatively good mark. However, this defeats the object of the module and would not be tolerated in the industry, where colour stories need to be accurate in terms of consumer acceptability and well defined. The workshop activities in this book aim to redress the shortfall of information delivered to the student or novice forecaster and encourage creative development of the understanding of the process. They will help you to understand the application of the process through a hands-on approach and will be of benefit on many other design modules.

Researching and initial data sourcing

Novice trend forecasters need to develop knowledge using observation, awareness and basic research techniques. Students may be shown previous students' work, which is of great benefit if its strengths and weaknesses are discussed to help establish benchmarks for standards. Never be tempted to copy the work of other people however; it should only ever be used as inspiration. The object is for you to develop your own ideas and expand your creativity and abilities. An interesting project for a trend prediction module would be to take a former student's project as a mock trend prediction package from a previous season. Using the colour forecasting tools and the principles of colour evolution, direction and rate of change you could produce a follow-on colour story, just as the colour forecasters do. This could also be applied to professional trend prediction packages: select one to analyse and follow it on with your own colour prediction.

Workshop activity

Getting to grips with colour evolution, direction of change, rate of change, and identifying moods through analysis and evaluation of past and present trend information are essential aspects of colour forecasting. Visit your library on a regular basis to keep abreast of new trends through trend prediction packages and trade magazines. Add notes and colour samples whenever possible to your portfolio.

Professional trend packages are an essential source of research and initial data sourcing and are available in most academic libraries. Trend packages are a valuable source of inspiration and information and to get the most from them you must return to them periodically to help establish a database. Through this information you will become more aware of the colour ranges and moods predicted for recent times and for the near future. This is of course an important source for historical trend research. Novices should also make themselves aware of the current colours and moods on the high street and be alert to what the general public is wearing.

Workshop activity

Developing awareness and observation skills. Visit high street stores on a regular basis to keep up to date with the colour stories being promoted. Researching individual retail companies to understand their consumer or target market will help you to understand the relevance of their colour stories. Also be aware of what colours people are wearing. Add notes and if possible colour samples to your portfolio.

Spinners' shade cards, trade and exhibition colour cards and forecasting service websites are all excellent sources for developing an initial database and appreciation of trend evolution. However, please remember that colours on the computer screen and print-outs from web-sites may not be an accurate representation of the intended colours, as discussed in Chapter 3.

It is interesting to note here how spinners use trend information to compile their shade cards. We found that in general, yarn manufacturers use trend prediction information for guidance and inspiration. This sector of the industry tends to keep sales data very much in mind when compiling or reviewing their colour ranges. Colours that sell well remain within the range; colours not selling at all or very little will be discontinued and replaced by new shades. Trend prediction packages are used to help the product range developer or designer decide which shades to add. Basically, colours in a trend prediction range similar to those already retained by the company and those similar to shades being discontinued will be ignored. Concentration will be on colours different to those already on the company's shade cards. The designer then uses an intuitive process of selection and elimination, choosing shades that work well with their remaining colour palette and which they feel their customers will like.

The colour palette will frequently appear uninspiring due to the favoured colours of their customers. Measures are often taken to include fashionable colours to brighten up the shade cards, making them more interesting to view. These additional colours are rarely expected to sell. Is this because the selection process is at fault? Or is it because the trend prediction information does not reflect consumer demand? Or because something more than intuition or guesswork is required?

Workshop activity

How much do spinners' shade cards reflect the trend predictions for the same season? Take a yarn or fabric company's shade card to your library to cross-reference with a trend prediction package for the same season and assess the similarities and differences in moods, staple and fashion colours in terms of hue, intensity and value. Do you feel that the manufacturing sector has used trend information effectively?

The brief

A brief is a structured set of criteria to be applied to a given task. The task itself is set out and the required results of that task are described. Forecasters, designers, buyers or anyone working within the role of trend prediction will be given a brief to work from for each season. Fashion and textile design students also work from a brief, imitating the activities of the industry.

On receipt of the brief, research should commence. Particularly for the novice, this should begin with an evaluation of current and past trend information. You should be making yourself aware of trend prediction information for the present and near future, with ideally four to six seasons of information. This is knowledge that forecasters would be aware of through both memory (if they have worked in the field long enough) and hard data from previous trend prediction packages. Forecasters feel that experience is a vital aspect of their role but gaining experience can be problematic for the novice. A research portfolio of trend information is an excellent way to prove that you are developing these essential skills, even though not yet working in the field of forecasting.

Role play

Design modules often use role play as a fundamental part of learning. This is an ideal way for the novice to feel the experience of being involved in the trend prediction sector. Students may be instructed to work alone or in teams; smaller class sizes tend to favour the former. Typically, the roles are as the initial forecasters, working for the specialist service sector; as designers working within the role of trend information user; or product range developers for a company. The work to be produced for the assignments will reflect the role the student is playing. For example, a student in the role of an individual working for or owning a forecasting company is likely to have to produce four or five mood boards and a professionally designed prediction package. Students taking the role of a designer for a company may have to produce one or more mood boards to show the colour range and to set the mood or theme, as well as a collection of styles or designs packaged to a professional standard. Students working in the role of yarn developers may have to create a colour range and design a trade fair stand to promote the company's new colour range. All of these roles and the resulting work reflect what goes on in the industry and tasks that the student may be involved in at some point in their future careers.

Packages

In order for the forecasting services to sell their ideas, their prediction packages become their marketing tool. Creativity and novelty become an integral part of the package design to sell the colour story predictions. Presentation skills are therefore a vital aspect for this sector of the industry and considered as important as the development of the colour stories themselves. Novices should be encouraged to be aware of the professionalism of the design of their own packages. It is important to consider whether the prime task is to develop their own design and presentation skills, or to understand the process of developing colour stories with confidence and accuracy and to achieve the right balance between the two.

Workshop activity

Select a range of trend prediction packages in your library and assess the visual aspects. Are they interesting? Does any company excel in their design and presentation? Do you have any ideas to suggest improvements? Evaluate other types of packaging, such as for gift items. Are there any novel ideas you could use as inspiration for the design of your own packaging?

Forecasting services need to be capable of selling their trend ideas though the mood boards and creativity should still play an important part in this task. If students have not yet acquired these skills and are not taught them on the module, they will be at a great disadvantage in the forecasting profession.

Developing colour stories

Now that we have a better understanding of how students are taught trend prediction and how the individual can add to this basic knowledge, we can apply all we have learnt so far about the colour forecasting process to the task of developing colour ranges or stories. We shall learn more about the techniques involved in designing mood boards and the presentation skills required, as well as about the different approaches to this through thought, reasoning and decision-making processes.

The process of colour forecasting is a seasonal challenge to be tackled with a colour story; the task of the forecaster is to develop a convincing one that reflects the desires of the consumer for a given season. The forecaster presents the colour story to the information user, most likely in a visual format, i.e. the prediction package and/or a verbal presentation. The key factor is how convincing the colour story is as a predictive tool for the industry in terms of accurately assessing consumer demand that will, in turn, result in a high volume of sales.

Approach to the task

Students effectively work from the same available sources of information, i.e. current and past trend prediction packages, current magazines and high street trends, and set to work using the same brief and criteria, yet we identified distinctive variations in working, thinking and problem-solving methodologies, as well as different end results. These differences revolve around the thought, reasoning and decision-making that are the underlying factors in the compilation of colour stories.

Students are given a brief to work from; colour forecasters also work to a set brief, though this may simply be the given season. Usually companies will have their own criteria for the number of colours in a range and the number of themes they need to produce. An overall theme may be decided upon and the company will be restricted by the markets they supply; such as womenswear, menswear, childrenswear, knitwear, lingerie, etc. Students are usually encouraged from the start to develop innovative ideas for the final presentation of the mood boards and trend prediction packages. A professional design would always be part of the forecaster's brief. Students may also consider the target market, consumer lifestyle and/or a company image. Again, for the forecaster, these factors would already be in place, however, they may feel the need to review such criteria particularly if they move or expand into other market niches.

We found that, on the whole, students do not use the observation and awareness skills of the forecaster when approaching the task of the colour story, even when the module is specifically concerned with trend prediction. Being aware of the colours currently available on the high street and colours predominantly worn by the general public are very important aspects of forecasting. If you have worked through the workshop activities in this chapter so far, you will have a good understanding of these tools and will be well on your way to developing them.

Thought, decision and reasoning processes

Intuition generally plays a large part in the thought and decision processes, and sparks inspiration. We found that almost 80% of students demonstrate initial inspiration for theme ideas in an intuitive manner, using thought, decision and reasoning processes at this early stage. Sourcing and data collection undoubtedly provide the stepping stones for initial inspiration, though students tend to disregard the importance of using previous trend prediction information. Remember, the key to colour forecasting is to identify the direction of change, and the rate and the timing of this change. To do this you must be aware of the colours already acceptable to the general public and the trend predictions following on from this season into the near future.

Two initial inspiration sources for developing a colour story have been identified: those that are thought inspired and those that are data inspired. Data may be used to support thought inspired ideas or be initial sources of inspiration themselves. An unlimited number of thought and resource information processes may be employed before the colour story is complete.

We found that initial inspiration can be directed either by thought or previous knowledge, or by visual stimuli. The professional forecaster uses a combination of both, with the relative percentage of each relating to experience obtained over the years. Figure 6.2 shows two methods of initial inspiration; the first being thought inspired leading to a controlled

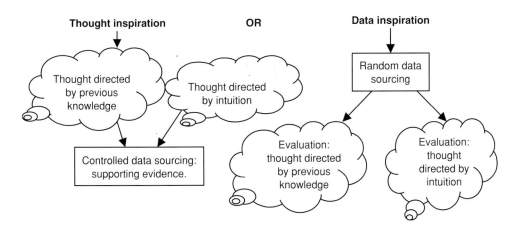

Figure 6.2 Initial inspiration sources.

method of data collection, to be used as supporting evidence for the original idea(s); and the second data inspired, where a random method of data sourcing is employed and thought processes – emotive or otherwise – are used for selection and/or elimination.

We investigated the approaches used by students on a number of relevant modules. We found that more than 60% of the students used thought as their initial inspiration, of whom nearly 90% started with previous knowledge as the basis for their thought processes. The remainder used visual stimuli as their initial inspiration after a random collection of data. All students tend to use their intuition as the basis for filtering the information into themes.

The initial inspiration may be thought or visually inspired, though once the thought, decision and reasoning processes begin and a direction or idea is decided upon, then further data collection and thought processes will become more controlled and more defined. However, even in the process of collecting data in a more controlled manner, there is the possibility of finding a random source of inspiration that may eventually be rejected or used to replace an existing idea. It is therefore the thought, decision and reasoning processes that are used to filter through the possibilities and to bring together a colour story that the student is satisfied with. The visual stimuli that came about either as initial inspiration or as supporting evidence, depending upon the route (i.e. thought inspired or visual data inspired), eventually becomes supporting evidence that initiates and promotes the colour story/colour prediction. Figure 6.3 demonstrates the cycle

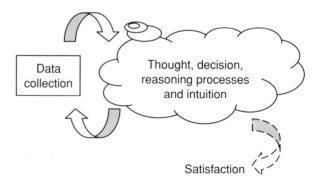

Figure 6.3 The process of data collection, thought, decision, reasoning and intuitive processes for selection and elimination purposes to reach a satisfactory result.

from the initial data collection stage, through to the compilation of the colour story and its presentation. These stages are reached once the individual is satisfied with the end result, after thought, decision and reasoning processes coupled closely with intuition.

There may be practical factors for selecting and eliminating data as well as purely intuitive reasons. A common reason is when the individual fails to source relevant data required to support preconceived ideas or themes. The revision of theme ideas may be necessary to solve this problem or random data collection may be used to initiate a fresh idea, with intuition helping to redefine them. Another common difficulty can occur when trying to match fabrics and yarns to colour stories compiled from imagery collected. Knowledge of craft-related subjects is of great benefit, as is a good knowledge of colour and CAD packages, in order to adjust both media and actual samples to produce the colours required. This would obviate the limitations of media available at the time, when the creative designer/forecaster wishes to promote something fresh.

Colour story workshop

We shall now work through a typical brief that forecasters may be required to follow in order to produce trend predictions or colour stories in the form of mood boards. Throughout this workshop exercise the methodology and thought/decision processes are set out to help you understand the practicalities of colour story development.

The brief

Using the title 'Mother Earth', compile a trend prediction colour story comprising 8 to 12 colours for an up-market ladies fashion boutique in a semi-rural market town. Design a mood board to show the predicted colour range for a season following on from the spring/summer colour palette given in Figure 6.1, demonstrating a high professional standard of presentation. Before embarking on this exercise, it is advisable to look at the final board, shown in Figure 6.10, on p. 150.

Initial data sourcing

To avoid any copyright restrictions, all materials reproduced for this workshop exercise are our own photography, art-work and natural, tangible samples. When producing mood boards or story boards for private use, these restrictions do not apply. Students and practising forecasters are able to use printed media such as imagery from magazines, greeting cards, gift wrap, etc, though this type of media should only be used for inspiration for the individual's own art and/or craft work. The use of original material on story boards is always recommended.

This colour range should be a follow-on from the spring/summer range shown in Figure 6.1 in order to demonstrate the processes used by the colour forecaster. The new colour range will therefore be for an autumn/winter season in the near future. The colours, their evolution and the mood of the previous range will be kept in mind while sourcing the data. The actions and thought processes are given informally, in personal note form, in stages to show the development and presentation of the board.

Stage 1

Thought inspiration – Mother Earth – what imagery does the title conjure up? An imaginary feminine form, who nurtures the Earth and all its produce. Keywords: natural, fertility, of the Earth, i.e. landscapes, foliage, vegetation, minerals.

Random data collection search, bearing in mind the title and keywords – looked in personal collection box of previously sourced data then scouted around the home and garden for relevant items as listed below (with their locations):

- a bowl of pot pourri (bedroom)
- bunch of corn (kitchen)
- bunch of lavender (kitchen)
- sea shells (bathroom)
- 3 pebbles (garden)
- rose leaves (leftovers from fresh flower arrangement)
- empty seed pack (collection box – a reminder for photos or live samples of flowers/foliage)
- rose quartz (collection box)
- rose quartz on a leather necklace (bedroom)
- rose drawer fragrance sachet with roses and butterfly print (collection box)

- crystal necklace (collection box)
- 2 coins (purse – representing 'of the Earth' – thought inspired)
- home-made papier mâché shell (collection box)
- wooden incense burner and incense sticks (bedroom)
- 3 landscape photos with sea views and mountain ranges (photo album)
- 3 woodland photos (photo album).

Stage 2

Process of selection/elimination – reassessment of what Mother Earth means, original keywords are still right, plus beauty. Looking at the items gathered, how fitting are they with the ideals?

- a bowl of pot pourri – keep: it's got lots of variety, colours and items, including rose buds; single out individuals pieces later
- bunch of corn – keep for now; it's nice and natural, can use single stalks instead of whole arrangement
- bunch of lavender – keep, same as for corn
- sea shells – pretty colours, still feel at this stage they are connected to title
- 3 pebbles – keep for now, natural
- rose leaves – keep, roses are synonymous with beauty and beautiful women, Mother Earth
- empty seed pack – don't want to use this as it is, keep on one side as a reminder to perhaps photograph some flowers/foliage
- rose quartz – keep, have more gemstones to add
- rose quartz on a leather necklace – decided to use the gemstones instead
- rose drawer fragrance sachet with roses and butterfly print – same as for empty seed pack
- crystal necklace – not sure; colours (reflected from facets) appear too bright, it's natural but doesn't look quite right! – have to reconsider it later
- 2 coins – definitely out of place, colour and item, eliminated!
- home-made papier mâché shell – not sure, keep for now as the sea shells have been kept
- wooden incense burner and incense sticks – originally selected to represent wood but it doesn't look natural, needs replacing with perhaps tree bark or twigs; eliminate but source some natural wood

- 3 landscape photos with sea views and mountain ranges – discarded, prefer to stick to the earth aspect rather than the sea; for this reason the shells may have to go too!
- 3 woodland photos – keep for now, possibly select one or two at the most; one shows a single red rose, fits with the pot pourri so this one will most likely stay.

Stage 3

In Stage 2 we narrowed down the ideas of what should constitute Mother Earth. Stage 3 – evaluation. Further sourcing was now more controlled, though random sourcing could still be employed. Thought: still feel that the crystal necklace is out of place, it could be replaced with a pearl necklace (bedroom), also collect more gemstones (lounge) and handmade paper for a background would be nice, not got any in collection box that feels right (intuitive thought regarding the aesthetics). The Mother Earth concept is now formulating very well. Further sourcing to be done in town – random, anything that is fitting with the title, keywords and items already collected. Controlled sourcing – handmade paper. Also want some wood, check garden or further afield (local countryside) if necessary.

Stage 4

Fruitless trip to town – saw some baskets but they were lacquered therefore lost their natural look. Spotted a silky cream scarf in a charity shop, but didn't really like the prints in the four corners even though they were country scenes with wild animals. However, it did inspire thought of a more natural looking silk scarf at home. Handmade paper in a closed shop window, have to go back another day! Had kebabs for tea then retrieved and washed the four wooden sticks, the scorch markings from the grill make the colouring quite interesting. Remembered to take photos of foliage/rockery in the garden, must get them developed!

Stage 5

Back to the board, at this stage we now have:

- a bowl of pot pourri
- bunch of corn

- bunch of lavender
- sea shells
- 3 pebbles
- rose leaves
- 2 photos of garden rockery
- rose quartz and additional gemstones
- pearl necklace – replacing the crystal necklace
- home-made papier mâché shell
- kebab sticks – replacing the wooden incense burner
- silk scarf
- 3 woodland photos.

Decided to draw a representation of Mother Earth (thought inspired) and add to the list of items. Particularly liked the garden photos, the terracotta pots link in well with the orange shades that were beginning to come through in the spring/summer colour range in Figure 6.1 which we are following on from. A live terracotta pot would be fitting (thought inspired) but can only find plastic flower pots around home/collection box – not natural looking; look around town when going for the handmade paper!

Stage 6

Further controlled data sourcing. Bought the handmade paper (gift shop) and a small terracotta pot (charity shop). Re-evaluation stage, placing all the items onto the handmade paper to make sure that all the items are fitting to the title and that the colours are all working well together. Another elimination process:

- a bowl of pot pourri
- bunch of corn – most likely use some of the stalks, not the whole arrangement
- bunch of lavender – same as corn
- sea shells – as the sea views have already been discarded the sea shells are now out of place; discard them!
- 3 pebbles – not happy with the colours, too dull; replaced with another stone (from the gemstone collection – lounge)
- rose leaves
- 2 photos of garden rockery
- rose quartz and additional gemstones – all discarded, too shiny, look out of place
- pearl necklace

- home-made papier mâché shell – discarded along with the sea shells
- kebab sticks
- silk scarf
- 3 woodland photos – too many, selected the one with the single red rose
- handmade paper
- terracotta pot
- Mother Earth figure (art work) – thought inspired.

The items were placed randomly on the paper to evaluate each piece within the concept as a whole. The pot pourri and the ivy growing up the wall behind the pots in the rockery photos inspired the thought of a pot pourri of yarns tumbling out of the terracotta pot and climbing up the board. Yarns of relevant colours in accordance with the colours of the items selected were sourced from the authors' extensive yarn store. Figure 6.4 shows a sketch of the initial layout of the selected items, including a small amount of selected interesting pieces from the bowl of pot pourri. The board was then disassembled in order to plan it out properly.

Figure 6.4 Sketch showing the initial layout of the selected items for the Mother Earth colour story board.

Stage 7

Planning the board. It was still possible at this stage to discard items and/or make additions. The list of items to be used is now:

- selected pieces of pot pourri – more pieces can be added if required
- bunch of corn – most likely use some of the stalks, not the whole arrangement
- bunch of lavender – same as corn
- purple stone
- rose leaves
- 2 photos of garden rockery
- pearl necklace
- kebab sticks
- silk scarf
- woodland photo showing a single red rose
- handmade paper
- terracotta pot
- Mother Earth figure
- pot pourri of selected yarn samples.

Planning the board layout

The mood board/story board should set a scene or tell a story to the viewer. The Mother Earth figure is the central inspiration, the direct link to the given title and therefore initially placed centrally on the paper. The next important sources of inspiration are the photos, these could have been imagery from magazines, etc., if the final board was not to be published. The inspirational focus of the board should be obvious to the viewer. Intuition prompts these core inspirations to be located in close proximity on the final board in this instance.

Mother Earth is an illusion. She appears out of the mists to take a brief step into reality, observing and giving succour to her Earth and its produce. The silk scarf is a representation of that mist, though more solid, more flowing, more feminine, soft and luxurious. The pearls are placed onto the scarf, these are gemstones one would imagine Mother Earth might wear. They are arranged as two heart shapes, one for her love for the Earth itself, the other for her love of all the Earth's produce. Mother Earth has been moved in closer to the mist and raised using a small piece of foam board, one foot is in the mist (under the scarf), while with the other she steps out into reality.

Figure 6.5 Sketch showing the first stage of development of the Mother Earth colour story board.

The woodland photo has been placed behind her, as she steps out of the mist and away from the natural woodland. The mist sweeps out of the bottom left hand corner of the board, melting away into the woodland image. Figure 6.5 shows the board's development to this stage.

The two garden photographs have been placed in front of the Mother Earth figure. She now seems to be stepping out from the natural woodland and into the garden, overseeing its care. At this stage some consideration was given to the title (thought inspired). Taking a rest from the board, different fonts, sizes and colours were experimented with on the computer until a decision was made (intuitively). The printed title was then roughly cut out and placed in the top left hand corner – may decide to move it later – also printed on tracing paper, as this allows the handmade paper to show through, most likely use this (thought). Figure 6.6 shows a sketch of the board to this stage.

Enlarged the photos of garden. Played around with cut out bits of photocopies until happy with result. Rockery cut outs lead from photo to purple stone. Rockery and terracotta pots cut out lead to terracotta pot. Didn't want collage pieces to look flat, raising them with foam board. Figure 6.7 shows the board layout at this stage.

Figure 6.6 Sketch showing the second stage of development of the Mother Earth colour story board.

Figure 6.7 Sketch showing the third stage of development of the Mother Earth colour story board.

Figure 6.8 Sketch showing the fourth stage of development of the Mother Earth colour story board.

Added two stalks of lavender, extending from the growth in the top garden photo. Thoughts: corn beginning to look out of place. Sticks – on photos, they come out of various plant pots, incorporate into the pot pourri of yarns planned to come from the terracotta pot. Lavender – coming from photo, looking at single rose in woodland photo; like to do same thing, take a rose from arrangement in lounge perhaps!

Arranged yarn pot pourri. Two sticks inserted for yarns to grow up. Added pieces of pot pourri intuitively, used much less than originally sorted. Figure 6.8 shows the development of the board so far.

Discarded purple stone – board looks cluttered, stone too heavy. Bits of pot pourri placed with yarns only. Earlier doubts about scarf returned. Thought: tissue paper, or something similar. Also use fake pearls from collection (originally overlooked) to replace real pearls. Colour slightly less interesting but need to mount the necklace, could paint the pearls to give them a more natural colouring.

Experimented with tracing paper, scrunching it up and opening it out. Decided to tear into three pieces to arrange in same shape as the scarf. Wondered if a transparent plastic bin bag would look better, tried it, experimented with the two combined, looks good – more natural mist-looking than the scarf. Added fake pearls, colour doesn't look too out of place against the new mist medium. Rearranged kebab sticks and pot in more upright position. Took off some pot pourri pieces to reduce busyness.

Want to add rose coming from woodland photo – moved title over more central to accommodate the rose to be added later. Interesting pot pourri dried flower inspired how to in-corporate the colour palette into the board. Sketched a flower head, photocopied using clone facility on copier – six per page, printed twice as 8–12 flowers are required according to the brief. Rough cut them out and placed on the mist – arranging and rearranging. Played around rearranging the fake pearls too – to be finalised on completion of mounting the board.

Added another stalk of lavender. Now ready to mount, and finalise colour palette. Like to use title printed on tracing paper – stick to handmade paper, but raised for interest and focus. Prepared to lose three to four inches off right-hand side of paper to use for this. This will reduce board size to approximately A2. Also decided to get terracotta pot cut through in half as it is too cumbersome and would be easier to mount one half.

Thought: board, either white and completely cover with handmade paper, or coloured leaving a border to frame the picture. Not got anything suitable in stock, have to go to town! Figure 6.9 shows the layout as planning thus far. The list of items to be used was to this stage:

- selected pieces of pot pourri – small amount used
- bunch of corn – discarded, out of place!
- 3 stalks of lavender
- purple stone – discarded, too heavy to mount and added to overall effect of the board being too heavy
- rose leaves – plus three dried rose buds from pot pourri
- 2 photos of garden rockery – plus 6 cut-outs from photocopies
- pearl necklace – fake
- 2 kebab sticks – reduced from 4
- silk scarf – replaced with tracing paper and transparent plastic bin bag
- woodland photo showing a single red rose
- handmade paper
- terracotta pot – to be cut through (from top to bottom) for easier mounting and to look less cumbersome
- Mother Earth figure
- pot pourri of selected yarn samples.

Figure 6.9 Sketch showing the fifth stage of development of the Mother Earth colour story board.

Colour Palette

Selected the prominent colours of the board, bearing in mind staple or main colours and accent or fashion colours. The strongly represented colours were:

- reds – roses and bricks in photos
- greens – grass and foliage in photos and rose leaves
- violet/blues – lavender, stones (rockery) and shadows in photos
- orange shades – terracotta pots (actual pot and cut-outs from the garden photos which were enlarged on the photocopier) and pot pourri pieces
- blues – stones in photos
- purple/pinks – bricks and shadows in photos
- cream – handmade paper and Mother Earth figure.
- off-white – pearls and mist.

All these colours, apart from the off-white, are supported in the colours of the pot pourri of yarns.

Singled out actual colours – considered different media – decided on acrylic paints for optimum colour matching and personal preference. Experimented with 26 colours – selected ten good matches. Painted onto watercolour paper as it is strong and slightly textured.

Mounting and final presentation

Cut board to A2 size. Trimmed handmade paper by wetting a line with water on a paint brush, used ruler as an edge and pulled paper away to leave a relatively straight but naturally uneven edge. Pasted in place with stick glue and double-sided tape, leaving a border of approximately $^1/_2$ cm of mounting board to frame. Decided mist was too heavy looking, wanted more of an accent than a feature – removed the tracing paper, leaving just the bin bag. Stuck in place with double-sided tape – no show through! Stuck photocopies and Mother Earth figure onto white card using stick glue to give body and strength and mounted on small pieces of foam board to raise.

Decided pearls were too heavy to mount and looked too much on the softer mist – cut individual pearls, using 12 mounted randomly with small pieces of pot pourri on the mist with a strong clear glue. Softened the straight edges of the photos by applying rough torn strips of handmade paper, glued in place with stick glue, blending torn edges into photos and background paper.

Mist now too small for complete colour palette – decided to mount coloured flowers around the top right corner of board and down right-hand side, using double-sided tape. Mounted pot, yarns, pot pourri dried flowers, rose buds and leaves with strong clear glue. Used stick glue to adhere tracing paper title to strip of handmade paper with rough torn edges approximately $^1/_2$ cm border, raised on foam board and added two halves of kebab stick beneath for extra interest. Made use of a few pieces of pot pourri around the board intuitively using strong clear glue.

Figure 6.10 shows the completed board for this workshop exercise. Figures 6.11, 6.12 and 6.13 show three other well designed mood boards we developed demonstrating high presentation skills. Some of the imagery on these older boards are not our own work but sourced some years ago from magazines, wallpaper and greeting cards.

Figure 6.10 Photograph of the completed Mother Earth workshop colour story board.

Figure 6.11 Photograph of a colour story board entitled Roses and Castles.

Figure 6.12 Photograph of a colour story board entitled Fantasy.

Figure 6.13 Photograph of a colour story board entitled Rocks and Minerals.

Summary

Colour forecasting is a process of continually sourcing data through a controlled or random manner in conjunction with thought, decision and reasoning processes that bring about the final colour story, to anticipate colour preferences of the consumer for a given season in the near future. It has been established that the process of developing a colour story is in part subjective and part objective. We found that the subjective tools of forecasting are more in evidence than the objective ones, even though these soft tools are generally little understood by forecasters, or even consciously used by them.

The professional forecaster automatically makes use of the soft, subjective tools. We feel that students should be more aware of these tools and encouraged to use them, otherwise design ideas could become isolated and not fit in with the marketing considerations.

In this chapter

The working methodology of the colour forecaster was further investigated through the development of a colour storyboard workshop exercise. The thought and decision-making processes were discussed and then applied to the workshop to assist an understanding of the forecasting process as applied to colour range development. Teaching methods of the colour forecasting process were discussed.

There is enormous opportunity for improvement in this area of study and including colour knowledge would be of great benefit to both students and professionals wishing to understand colour forecasting. We strongly recommend carrying out the workshop activities in this chapter and in Chapter 3 to enhance learning.

7 The future of colour forecasting

Forecasters form a specialist sector that has developed through the growth of the fashion and textile industry. Before this, manufacturers took inspiration from *haute couture*. As *haute couture* styling became increasingly impractical (as a result of its attempts to separate itself from the ready-to-wear industry), its designs became less important as an inspirational source. The specialist forecasting sector was established to relieve the manufacturers of the process of sourcing for inspiration – which had become more complex due to the wide range of consumer lifestyle choices now available. While forecasting is primarily a specialist sector activity, every manufacturing company and retailer in the industry carries out forecasting at some level themselves. Some companies – particularly independent retailers – do not subscribe to a forecasting service and profess to work entirely intuitively. However, even these employ a method of forecasting not entirely dissimilar to that of the specialist sector, using forecast information primarily as a source of inspiration rather than a prescription.

In this chapter

We shall summarise:

- what the reader has learnt throughout this book
- how this book contributes to existing published material
- some possible areas for further investigation.

What you have learnt from this book

In Chapter 1 we looked back to the onset of the industrial revolution in order to understand how, when and why the need for forecasting came about, and how it has evolved to its current state. We outlined how the fashion and textile industry developed and increased in capacity, as higher production speeds and quality of end products were easily achievable and provided a mass of ready-to-wear garments at prices affordable to all. Previously, fashionable garments were handmade, bespoke, by skilled designers, tailors and seamstresses. The garments were expensive, as were the imported fabrics they used, which made fashion exclusive to the wealthy.

As the fashion and textile industry grew, garments produced for the mass population could no longer be made individually for the client. Manufacturers found it increasingly difficult to assess the needs of the consumer and to make products they felt confident would sell.

The growth of the manufacturing industry increased competition between companies and as the retail industry also increased in capacity, competition on the high street rose. Consumers were beginning to show sophistication in their choices and with the wide range of retail outlets now available, retailers began to employ marketing techniques to tailor their stores to a particular clientele. Retailers started to recognise and understand their target customers' needs and desires and dictated their stores' requirements to the manufacturers. While there are still many manufacturers selling direct to warehouses who retail from their own premises, most manufacturers now produce to order, on the demands of the large retailers.

The need for forecasting first became evident around 1825 when British manufacturers visited the USA for inspiration. This need had increased by the third decade of the twentieth century and had very much intensified by the 1970s as manufacturing had to become much more focused on what the consumer wanted to order to ensure profitability. Colour is an easy aspect of a design to alter cost effectively, giving a fresh look to an otherwise dated style. This can offer more 'mileage' from a single design as the manufacturing specifications need little or no alteration and the production workers remain familiar with the making-up techniques, both reducing mistakes and the time required to learn new procedures. This, coupled with the fact that colour is very influential in the consumer's decision to purchase, has meant that colour and the accurate forecasting of colour preferences has now become of major importance to the fashion and textile industry.

In Chapter 2 we learnt about the importance of colour forecasting for the fashion and textile industry, the methodology used to develop colour ranges and how this information is used. This was approached primarily through an evaluation of current published material and through discussions with key personnel in the industry. We looked closely at the colour forecasting process by developing models of both the current process and a suggested improved process, which was extensively scrutinised by the industry as described in Chapter 4.

We examined the soft tools used in forecasting in Chapter 5 in order to understand aspects such as intuition and inspiration, as well as thought, reasoning and decision-making processes. We found, through our research, that the colour knowledge of students on the fashion and textile design courses studied was lower than what the role of colour trend forecasting and other design related roles requires. To help redress this lack of knowledge, Chapter 3 was designed to give the reader both information and practical experience through workshop activities. This combination continued into Chapter 6, where the reader was encouraged to develop a trend prediction portfolio to reflect their own study into this area, as well as to help to understand the colour forecasting process more clearly.

Chapter 6 brought together all the aspects of colour forecasting discussed in the book with a worked example of colour story board development and guidance on achieving a high standard of presentation.

This book's contribution

Primary research and other investigations were conducted by the authors with UK degree students on fashion and related textile design courses to investigate the teaching methods used in trend prediction modules and to asses how students develop their forecasting skills. Due to the lack of in-depth information available to the student and lecturer, teaching methods were found to be limited, leaving the student to develop their own methodology, based on a mix of unverified evidence and intuition. Both individual students and teams were involved in the exercises to better understand the thought and decision-making processes adopted when developing a colour story, or range.

A form of soft systems methodology proved useful for the development of the conceptual models – one of the current colour forecasting system and one of a proposed improved system, taking into account consumer desired, or preference colour data. Both models were refined using information obtained from personnel within the fashion and textile industry who responded to questionnaires. A high percentage of the respondents of this survey felt that the first model was an accurate representation of the current system. It was also agreed that the industry as a whole would benefit from improvements to the current system, especially the inclusion of consumer colour desired data.

The authors also found that the current system was not satisfying the consumer to the degree that the forecasters claim, and that consumers and the industry would derive immediate benefit from forecasting using consumer colour preference data. Though it was appreciated that it could be even more beneficial to specify to the consumer what particular items of clothing the proposed colours would be applied to, as certain colours may be considered acceptable for perhaps a blouse but not for a trouser suit.

This book has helped you understand that:

- the driving forces of fashion have always primarily been concerned with the consumer, though the nature of the consumer has changed throughout time
- colour is an important driving force of fashion today, from the manufacturer's viewpoint and the consumer's
- there is a strong need for a deeper knowledge and understanding of the colour forecasting process for students and the newcomer to the fashion and textile industry, and consequently a more effective teaching method of the process.

Further possible improvements to the current colour forecasting process

We have in this book recognised that the current colour forecasting process could be improved by the introduction of consumer colour preference data.

Bringing consumer opinion more effectively into colour forecasting suggests two possible approaches. The direct approach would require real data to be registered, quantified and analysed. This data would have to be generated by tedious and time-consuming surveying and its accuracy would always be in question. Electronic technology could however be used in stores to collect data, or specially designed question-naires and games could be placed in fashion magazines and catalogues.

The second approach would need research to more accurately deduce the affective or emotional issues related to colour. Much valuable research is now being conducted into the measurable emotional effects of colour. If its results are verified and published, it will be important for colour forecasters to be aware and make use of them.

Looking to the future of colour forecasting, we offer two suggestions. First, the teaching of the colour forecasting process in fashion and textile related degrees could be greatly improved. This book will hopefully provide a platform for further investigation of the current teaching process and potential improvements. Second, the perception and assess-ment of colour by individuals could be examined, along with the systems currently used for communicating colour, and suggested improvements to those systems.

In this chapter

We summarised the knowledge that you have gained through this book and its importance in adding to the current body of knowledge of colour forecasting or colour trend prediction. We concluded this chapter with suggestions for future invest-igation in the hope of encouraging further study and an ever-changing and improving system of forecasting for the fashion and textile industry to benefit from. It is our intention to encourage a higher standard of teaching and learning of this and related subject areas.

We found that much of the colour forecasting process is based upon subjective tools such as intuition, inspiration and creativity. These aspects in general were considered to be little understood in themselves. This book has attempted to reveal their meanings and better understand their application in the forecasting process. Although the aims and objectives of this book have been to demystify and clarify the process, there was no intention on the part of the authors to deny the importance of intuition and inspiration which can be optimised by the addition of an effective forecasting process. While we endorse the need for intuition, inspiration and creativity, we consider that there is a need for more research in this area.

And finally

Colour is all around us; try to further your understanding and appreciation of it. Collect and store samples whenever you see an attractive or interesting colour, adding to your personal portfolio and keep up to date with whatever tools you find most useful. Above all, enjoy it!

Bibliography

Armstrong, T., 1991. *Colour Perception*. Tarquin Publishers, UK.

Barthes, R., 1983. *The Fashion System*. Hill & Wang, New York.

Barton, A., 1984. *The Rise and Fall of the Cotton King*. Jolly & Barber, UK.

Baudot, F., 1999. *A Century of Fashion*. Thames & Hudson, London.

BBC Video, 1991. *The Colour Eye*.

Benson, L., Bruce, M., Oulton, D., & Hogg, M. K. c. 1999. *The Colour Conspiracy: A summary of colour forecasting in the textile clothing industry and its influence on future predictions for a UK mail order company*. UMIST, Manchester (conference paper).

Berstresser, G. A. III, 1984. *Textile Marketing Management*. Noyes Publications, USA.

Birren, F. (Ed.), 2001. *Itten: The Elements of Colour*. John Wiley, Canada.

Birren, F., 1978. *Colour and Human Response*. Van Nostrand Reinhold, USA.

Birren, F., 1961. *Colour Psychology and Colour Therapy*. Citadel, Secausus, New Jersey.

Bond, D., 1988. *The Guinness Guide to Twentieth Century Fashion*. Guinness Publishing, London.

de Bono, E., 1996. *De Bono's Thinking Course*. BBC Worldwide Publishing, London.

Bradfield, N., 1985. *Costume in Detail 1730–1930*. Harrap, England.

Brannon, E. L., 2000. *Fashion Forecasting*. Fairchilds Publications, Inc., New York.

Briscoe, L., 1971. *The Textile and Clothing Industries*. The University Press, Manchester.

Buddy, J., 1992. *A Slave to Fashion? Fashion & Colour Trends in the 1990s – Forecasting the Future*. Journal of the Society of Dyers & Colourists, Vol. 108.

Burns, L. Davis, 2002. *The Business of Fashion: Designing, Manufacturing and Marketing*. 2nd Edition. Fairchilds Publications, New York.

Burns, L. D., & Bryant, N., 1997. *The Business of Fashion*. Fairchilds Publications, New York.

Bush, S., 1987. *The Silk Industry*. Shire Publications Ltd, England.

Byrd, P., 1992. *A Visual History of Costume: The Nineteenth Century*. B. T. Batsford, London.

Byrne, A., & Hilbert, D. R. (Eds), 1997. *Readings on Colour*. MIT Press, UK.

Callan, G. O'Hara, 1998. *The Thames & Hudson Dictionary of Fashion and Fashion Designers*. Thames & Hudson, London.

Carlin International. Richmond Bridge House, Twickenham.

Carr, H., & Latham, B., 1994. *The Technology of Clothing Manufacture*. Blackwell Publishing, Oxford.

Carter, E., 1980. *Magic Names of Fashion*. Weidenfield & Nicholson, London.

Chamberlain, J., & Quilter, J. H., 1924. *Common Commodities and Industries: Knitted Fabrics*. Pitman & Sons Ltd, London.

Chamberlin, E. R., 1976. *The Awakening Giant: Britain in the Industrial Revolution*. B. T. Batsford, London.

Channel 4 Video, 1998. *Undressed : Fashion in the Twentieth Century.*

Checkland, P. B., 1981. *Systems Thinking, Systems Practice*. John Wiley, USA.

Checkland, P. B., & Sproles, J., 1990. *Soft Systems Methodology in Action*. John Wiley, USA.

Chiazzari, S., 1998. *The Complete Book of Colour*. Element Books, UK.

Chrisolm, R. K., & Whittaker, G. R., 1972. *Forecasting Methods*. Richard D. Irwin, Illinios.

Chrisnall, P. M., 1975. *Marketing: A Behavioural Analysis*. McGraw-Hill, UK.

Cohen, A., C., 1989. *Marketing Textiles from Fibre to Retail*. Fairchilds Publications, USA.

Cohen, J., 1972. *Psychological Probability, or the Art of Doubt*. George Allen & Unwin, London.

Colchester, C., 1991. *The New Textiles Trends and Traditions*. Thames & Hudson, London.

Coleman, E. A., 1989. *The Opulent Era: Fashions of Worth, Doucet & Pingat*. Thames & Hudson and The Brooklyn Museum, London.

Collezioni, Distribuzione in Italia Logos Art. Modena, Italy.

Colour Research and Application. John Wiley, New York.

Cook, G. J., 1984. *Handbook of Natural Fibres*. Merrow Publishing, England.

Cooklin, G., 1997. *Garment Technology for Fashion Designers*. Blackwell Science, Oxford.

Cumming, R., & Porter, T., 1990. *The Colour Eye*. BBC Books, London.

Danger, E. P., 1968. *Using Colour to Sell*. Gower Publishing, London.

Danger, E. P., 1987. *The Colour Handbook*. Gower Publishing, London.

Danger, E. P., 1987. *The Colour Handbook: How to use colour in commerce and industry*. Billing & Sons, UK.

Design Intelligence. Goodnews Press, UK.

Diamond, J., & Diamond, E., 1997. *The World of Fashion*. Fairchild Publications, USA.

Diamond, J., & Diamond, E., 1994. *Fashion Apparel and Accessories*. Delmar Publications, New York.

Dickerson, K. G., 1995. *Textiles and Apparel: In the Global Economy*, 2nd Edition. Prentice-Hall, New Jersey.

Dingemans, J., 1999. *Mastering Fashion Styling*. Macmillan Press, UK.

Docherty, C. A., Hann, M. A., & Schgor, K. V., 1999. *Stylistic Change in Womenswear Products – A Reappraisal.* De Montfort University, Leicester.

Drake, M. F., Spoone, J. Harrison, & Greenwald, H., 1992. *Retail Fashion Promotion and Advertising.* Macmillan Publishing, New York.

Drapers Record. *Expofil Trends, Autumn/ Winter 2003.* EMAP UK.

Drapers Record Centenary Supplement. August 1987. International Thomson Publishing, London.

Earl, P. P., & Kemp, S., 1999. *The Elgar Companion to Consumer Research and Economic Psychology.* Edward Elgard, Cheltenham.

Easey, M., 1995. *Fashion Marketing.* Blackwell Science, Oxford.

Easey, M., 2002. *Fashion Marketing*, 2nd Edition. Blackwell Publishing, Oxford.

Edelkoort, L., 1999. *The Theories Behind Colour Forecasting.* The Briggait Centre, Glasgow. October, 19th, 1999 (presentation).

Ellacott, S. E., 1956. *Spinning and Weaving.* Methuen & Co., Ltd, London.

English, W., 1969. *The Textile Industry.* W & J Mackay, UK.

Evans, R. M., 1974. *The Perception of Colour.* John Wiley, USA.

Ewing, A. F., 1972. *Planning and Policies in the Textile Finishing Industry.* Bradford University Press, UK.

Ewing, E., 1989. *Everyday Dress. 1650–1900.* B. T. Batsford, London.

Fashion Forecast International. Styleman, London.

Fashion Theory. The journal of dress, body and culture. Berg Publishers, Oxford.

Fearon, F., 1996. Trend Forecasting. *Knitting International.* Issue 1223, Vol. 103.

Fiore , A. M., & Kimle, P. A., 1997. *Understanding Aesthetics for the Merchandising & Design Professional.* Fairchilds Publications, New York.

Flugel, J. C., 1966. *The Psychology of Clothes.* Hogarth Press, London.

Foster, V., 1992. *A Visual History of Costume: The Twentieth Century.* B. T. Batsford, London.

Foxall, G., 1997. *Marketing Psychology.* Macmillan Press, UK.

Frings, G. S., 2002. *Fashion from Concept to Consumer.* 7th Edition. Prentice-Hall, New Jersey.

Frings, G. S., 1991. *Fashion from Concept to Consumer.* Prentice-Hall, New Jersey.

Fritz, A., & Cant, J., 1989. *Consumer Textiles.* Oxford University Press, UK.

Galliers, R. (Ed.), 1992. *Information Systems Research.* Blackwell Science, Oxford.

Garnham, A., & Oakhill, J., 1994. *Thinking & Reasoning.* Blackwell Science, Oxford.

Garthe, M., 1995. *Fashion and Colour.* Rockport Publishers Inc., MA:, USA.

Gilhooly, K. J., 1988. *Thinking: Directed, Undirected & Creative.* Academic Press, London.

Gimbell, T., 1980. *Healing Through Colour.* C.W. Daniel, USA.

Global Vision (Ed.), 1993. *United Colours of Benetton.* Robundo Publishing, Japan.

Godfrey, F. P., 1982. *An International History of the Sewing Machine.* Robert Hale Publishing, UK.

Gouras, P. (Ed.), 1991. *The Perception of Colour.* Macmillan Press, UK.

Goworek, H., 2001. *Fashion Buying.* Blackwell Publishing, Oxford.

Grace, E., 1978. *Introduction to Fashion Merchandising.* Prentice-Hall, USA.

Gray, S., 1998. *CAD/CAM in Clothing and Textiles.* The Design Council. Gower Publishing, UK.

Green, B., 1994. *An Investigation into the Decision Making Process used by Colourists within Clothing Fashion Prediction, with Special Reference to Women's Wear.* Royal College of Art, London.

Greenwood, K., Moore, & Murphy, M. Fox, 1978. *Fashion Innovation & Marketing.* Macmillan Publishing, New York.

Gross, R., & McIlveen, R., 1998. *Psychology: A New Introduction.* Hodder & Stroughton, UK.

Guerin, P., 1987. *Creative Fashion Presentations.* Fairchilds Publications, USA.

Guild, T., 1996. *Tricia Guild on Colour.* Conran Octopus, London.

Hann, M. A., & Jackson, K. C., 1985. *Fashion: An Interdisciplinary Review.* Vol. 16, no. 4, The Textile Institute, Manchester.

Hansen, H. H., 1975. *Costume Cavalcade.* Cox & Wyman, UK.

Harvey, M., 1998. The Fashion Soothsayers. *Drapers Record.* EMAP. July 11th.

de la Haye, A., & Wilson, E., 1999. *Defining Dress: Dress as Object, Meaning & Identity.* Manchester University Press, UK.

Healey, K. R., 1984/85. An Analysis of Forecasting and Fashion Services Available for Knitwear Manufacturers. *Knitting International.* Vol. 91, no. 1091 & 1092; Vol. 92, no. 1093–1096.

Hiers, B., 1987. *The Professional Decision Thinker.* Sidgwick & Jackson, London.

Hope, & Walsh, 1990. *The Color Compendium.* Van Nostrand Reinhold, USA.

Hudson, P. B., Clapp, A. C., & Kness, D., 1993. *Joseph's Introductory Textile Science,* 6th Edition. Holt, Rinehart & Winston, USA.

Hudson, N., 2001. A Meeting of Minds. *Prediction.* Vol. 67, no. 9.

Hulse, T., 1997. The Colour Conspiracy. *Hotline Magazine,* Meridian, Birmingham.

Hunter, R. S., & Harold, R. W. (Eds), 1987. *The Measurement of Appearance,* 2nd Edition. John Wiley, USA.

Hurlock, E. B., 1976. *The Psychology of Dress.* Arnos Press, New York.

International Textiles, 1992. *Behind the Scenes at Premier Vision. The Story Unfolds.* Grange Press, Vol. 731.

International Textiles, 1991. *World Review of Textile Design.* Grange Press, Vol. 725.

International Textiles, 1988. *Predicting the Future of Fashion Prediction.* Grange Press, Vol. 689.

Itten, J., 1961. *The Art of Colour.* Van Nostrand Reinhold, New York.

Jabanis, E., 1983. *The Fashion Directors: What they do and how to be one.* John Wiley, Canada.

Jacques, B., 1994. *The Complete Colour, Style and Image Book.* Thorsons, London.

Jarnow, J., & Dickerson, K. G., 1997. *Inside the Fashion Business,* 6th Edition. Prentice-Hall, New Jersey.

Jarnow, J. A., Judelle, B., & Guerreiro, M., 1981. *Inside the Fashion Business.* John Wiley, USA.

Jenkins, D. T. (Ed.), 1994. *The Textile Industries.* Blackwell Science, Oxford.

Jorgensen, D. L., 1989. *Participant Observation: A Method for Human Studies.* Sage Publications, USA.

Jung, C. G., 1956. *The Integration of Personality.* Routledge & Kegan Paul, London.

Jenkins, D. T. (Ed.), 1994. *The Textile Industries.* Blackwell Science, Oxford.

Kennet, F., 1983. *The Collector's Book of Twentieth Century Fashion.* Granada Publishing, UK.

Killick, K., & Schaverien, J. (Eds), 1997. *Art, Psychotherapy and Psychosis.* Routledge, London.

Kirby, N., 1994. *Colour Forecasting: An Analysis of Trends in Women's Apparel.* UMIST, Manchester.

Kleinke, C. L., 1978. *Self Perception: The Psychology of Personal Awareness.* W. H. Freeman, San Francisco.

Kline, P., 1993. *Personality: The Psychometric View.* Routledge, London.

Konig, R., 1973. *A La Mode: On the Psychology of Fashion.* George Allen & Unwin, USA.

Lambert, E., 1976. *World of Fashion.* R. R. Bowker, New York.

Lambert, P., Staepelaere, B., & Fry, M. G., 1986. *Colour and Fibre.* Schifter Publishing, Pennsylvania.

Laver, J., 1937. *Taste and Fashion.* George G. Harrap, London.

Laver, J., 1966. *Dress (The Changing Shape of Things Series).* John Murray, London.

Lehnert, G., 1999. *Fashion: A Concise History.* Laurence King Publishers, London.

Libby, W. C., 1974. *Colour & the Structural Sense.* Prentice-Hall, New Jersey.

Linton, H., 1994. *Colour Consulting – A Survey of International Colour Design.* Van Nostrand Reinhold, New Jersey.

Lister, M., 1977. *Costumes of Everyday Life.* Barrie & Jenkins, London.

Luscher, M. & Scott, I. (Eds), 1970. *The Luscher Colour Test.* Jonathon Cape, London.

Malossi, G. (Ed.), 1998. *The Style Engine.* The Monacelli Press, USA.

McGoldrick, P. J., 1990. *Retail Marketing.* McGraw-Hill Publishing, England.

Mendes, V., & de la Haye, A., 1999. *Twentieth Century Fashion.* Thames & Hudson, London.

Merrett, R., 1997. The Colours of Nelly Rodi. *International Textiles* (vol. 798), Grange Press, UK.

Meyers, L. S., & Grossen, N. E., 1974. *Behavioral Research: Theory, Procedure and Design.* W. H. Freeman, USA.

Nassau, K. (Ed.), 1998. *Colour for Science, Art and Technology.* Elsevier, UK.

Nelly Rodi. Distributed by Lynette Southall & Associates, London.

Nemcsics, A., 1993. *Colour Dynamics: Environmental Colour Design.* Ellis Horwood, UK.

Patching, D., 1990. *Practical Soft Systems Analysis.* Pitman Publishing, London.

Peacock, J., 1977. *Fashion Sketch Book: 1920–60.* Thames & Hudson, London.

Peacock, J., 1993. *20th Century Fashion.* Thames & Hudson, London.

Peacock, J., 1997. *Fashion Sourcebooks: The 1930s.* Thames & Hudson, London.

Peacock, J., 1998. *Fashion Sourcebooks: The 1940s.* Thames & Hudson, London.

Peacock, J., 1997. *Fashion Sourcebooks: The 1950s.* Thames & Hudson, London.

Peacock, J., 1998. *Fashion Sourcebooks: The 1960s.* Thames & Hudson, London.

Peacock, J., 1997. *Fashion Sourcebooks: The 1970s.* Thames & Hudson, London.

Peacock, J., 1998. *Fashion Sourcebooks: The 1980s.* Thames & Hudson, London.

Pearce, C., 1971. *Prediction Techniques for Marketing Planners.* Ebenezeer Baylis & Son, UK.

Perna, R., 1987. *Fashion Forecasting.* Fairchilds Publications, USA.

Perrot, P., translated by R. Bienvenu, 1994. *Fashioning the Bourgeois: A History of Clothing in the Nineteenth Century.* Princeton University Press, New Jersey.

de Poala, H. & Mueller, C. S., 1980. *Marketing Today's Fashion.* Prentice-Hall, New Jersey.

Ponting, K. G., 1981. *Discovering Textile History & Design.* Shire Publications, UK.

Pooser, D., 1986. *Always in Style.* Little Hills Press, UK.

Ramsey, J. B., 1977. *Economic Forecasting – Models or Markets?* The Institute of Economic Affairs, London.

Reid, L., 2000. *Colour Book.* Connections Book Publishing, London.

Reynolds, H., 1997. *Courture or Trade.* Phillimore, UK.

Ribeiro, A., 1983. *A Visual History of Costume: The Eighteenth Century*. Batsford, London.

Riley, C. A., 1995. *Colour Codes*. University Press of New England, USA.

Rouse, E., 1989. *Understanding Fashion*. Blackwell Science, Oxford.

Roweth, Z., 2000. (personal interview), 17th July.

van Someren, M. W., Barnard, Y. F., Sandberg., J. A. C., 1994. *The Think Aloud Method: A Practical Guide to Modelling Cognitive Processes*. Academic Press, London.

Sommer, R., & Sommer, B., 1997. *A Practical Guide to Behavioral Research Tools and Techniques*. Oxford University Press, New York.

Spillane, M., 1991. *The Complete Style Guide*. Piatkus Publishers, London.

Sproles, G. B., 1979. *Fashion: Consumer Behaviour Toward Dress*. Burgess Publishing, USA.

Sproles, G. B., & Burns, L. D., 1994. *Changing Appearances: Understanding Dress in Contempory Society*. Fairchilds Publications, USA.

Steele, V., 1997. *50 Years of Fashion: New Look to Now*. Yale University Press, USA.

Stevenson, P., 1980. *Edwardian Fashion*. Ian Allen, UK.

Stone, E., 1987. *Fashion Buying*. McGraw-Hill, USA.

Storey, J., 1992. *The Thames & Hudson Manual of Dyes and Fabrics*. Thames & Hudson, UK.

Tate, S. L., 1984. *Inside Fashion Design*, 2nd Edition. Harper & Row, New York.

Teevan, R. C., & Birney, R. C. (Eds), 1961. *Colour Vision*. Van Nostrand, Canada.

Textile History. Maney & Sons, UK.

Textile View, 1999, Metropolitan Publishing, The Netherlands.

Thompson, M., 1990. *Teach Yourself Philosophy*. Cox & Wyman, UK.

Tordoff, M., 1984. *A Servant of Colour: A History of the SDC 1884–1984*. Society of Dyers and Colourists, UK.

Tozer, J., & Levitt, S., 1983. *The Fabric Society: A Century of People and their Clothes 1770–1870*. Laura Ashley, UK.

Tse, K. K., 1985. *Marks & Spencer*. Pergaman Press, UK.

Tudor, D. J., & Tudor, I. J., 1995. *Systems Analysis and Design*. Blackwell Publishing, UK.

Turner, D., & Greco, T., 1998. *The Personality Compass*. Element Books, UK.

Tyrrell, A. V., 1986. *Changing Trends in Fashion*. Batsford, London.

Valentine, C. W., 1968. *The Experimental Psychology of Beauty*. Associated Book Publishers, London.

Vaughan, F. E., 1979. *Awakening the Intuition*. Anchor Books, New York.

View on Colour. United Publishers, France.

Watkins, P., 1992. *Interior Trends Interpretations & Predictions.* Textile Horizons International. Textile Institute, Manchester. Vol. 12, No. 2.

Weinberg, G., & Schmaker, J. A., 1969. *Statistics on Intuitive Approach.* Brooks Cole Publishing, USA.

White, D., 1998. *Success with Psychometric Testing.* Management Books, UK.

Whelan, B. M., 1994. *Colour Harmony: 2.* Thames & Hudson, London.

Wills, G., & Midgley, D., 1973. *Fashion Marketing.* George Allen & Unwin, UK.

Winters, A. A., & Goodman, S., 1984. *Fashion Advertising and Promotion.* Fairchilds Publications, New York.

Wong, W., 1997. *Principles of Colour Design.* Van Nostrand Reinhold, New York.

Worth, G., 2000. The Lineage of Colour Forecasting in the UK. *Art & Design Research Journal.* Issue 9.

Wright, A., 1998. *The Beginner's Guide to Colour Psychology.* Kyle Cathie, London.

Wright, G., & Goodwin, P., 1998. *Forecasting with Judgement.* John Wiley, UK.

Wright, W. D., 1969. *The Measurement of Colour*, 4th Edition. Adam Hilger, London.

Yarwood, D., 1992. *Fashion in the Western World.* Batsford, London.

Zelanski, P., & Fisher, M. P., 1989. *Colour.* The Herbert Press, London.

Index